'This is a much-needed book about a much-misunderstood topic. Told with humour and humanity, Jamie is a pioneer.'

Juno Dawson, columnist and author of
Wonderland *and* The Gender Games

'*In Their Shoes* by Jamie Windust is a magical, beautiful, heartbreaking and often hilarious memoir that should be CRUCIAL READING for everyone living in our world today. Jamie is an extraordinary voice and person and their book is one of the best I've read in a very, very long time. Not only does Jamie powerfully address the challenges faced by trans people who are just trying to live, they also delicately map their life in an artful and revolutionary way. For Jamie, the personal is political and the political is personal and this book is as heartbreaking as it is heartwarming. If you do one thing this month – read this book!'

Scarlett Curtis, writer, journalist, activist and curator of
It's Not OK to Feel Blue *and* Feminists Don't Wear Pink

'It always makes me so happy to see queer people tell their stories unapologetically, because it breaks the stigma that being queer is something to be ashamed of. Jamie's book is thought-provoking, funny, poignant and endlessly queer, and I'm here for it.'

Ugla Stefanía Kristjönudóttir Jónsdóttir (Owl),
co-director of My Genderation

'*In Their Shoes* doesn't tiptoe over fairy dust with a dainty ballet slipper. Jamie's heels clatter over tiled floors – loud enough to know they're coming and loud enough to know they mean business.'

Rhyannon Styles, author of
The New Girl *and ELLE columnist*

'A vibrant and illuminating read from a truly exciting mind – *In Their Shoes* is a love letter to our non-binary siblings.'

Paula Akpan, journalist

IN
THEIR
SHOES

*Navigating
Non-Binary Life*

Jamie Windust

Jessica Kingsley Publishers
London and Philadelphia

First published in Great Britain in 2021 by Jessica Kingsley Publishers
An Hachette Company

1

Author photo: Thomas Alexander for SHOWstudio

A CIP catalogue record for this title is available from the British Library
and the Library of Congress

ISBN 978 1 78775 242 9
eISBN 978 1 78775 243 6

Printed and bound in Great Britain by Clays Ltd.

Jessica Kingsley Publishers policy is to use papers that are natural,
renewable and recyclable products and made from wood grown in
sustainable forests. The logging and manufacturing processes are expected
to confirm to the environmental regulations of the country of origin.

Jessica Kingsley Publishers
73 Collier Street
London N1 9BE, UK

www.jkp.com

Contents

To Cat, for the endless calls and rambles, and for being the best friend I'd always dreamed of

To Jonnie, for being a friend and constant I never thought I'd be worthy of

To Andrew, for seeing something in me that I didn't know was able to flourish

To me, for beginning the journey of self-appreciation and acceptance of my own identity, something I never thought I'd be able to do

To you, my community, for never stopping

Someone Else's Shoes

I literally tried being in someone else's shoes once and it wasn't the most comfortable experience. Probably because it meant that I had to wear flat shoes for more than ten minutes, which is never a nice feeling. Too close to the ground. Too real. Every step you take is too close to the earth that supports us. Too close to the very thing that holds us steady, but also the thing that has the ability to collapse beneath us at any given moment, allowing us to fall to the centre. Allowing us to empathize with similar feelings. That feeling of absorbing someone else's time. The shape that they have carved out for themselves, with you sliding on top, not necessarily fitting exactly, but being able to feel that time has passed there. That memories, birthdays, deaths, happiness, terror have all happened for this person, in their shoes. But now you're wearing those shoes. You're in control of them, seeing the world from a fresh perspective. A perspective you might not know, and a perspective you might not like. But you're seeing it, and that's what's important.

I often think that we are in an empathy drought right now. In this current climate we are in, with the world and its news whirling past us constantly, world-wide global crises feel like they're happening just in the palm of our hands, but are in fact real, tangible, life-threatening moments that are happening somewhere on our planet. Once the next one comes through, beeping at us in the middle of the night, or catching our eye on the news screens when we are waiting at the train station, we forget what we were just feeling. We are the prizes in the claw-crane games at the arcade, swiftly being picked up from above and moved to another spot to witness a new piece of information that requires our full attention and our care, swiftly forgetting where we just were and acclimatizing to our new surroundings.

Trans people are often forgotten about for this very reason. I think, realistically, people prioritize problems that are happening to them, and subsequently prioritize other issues based on their proximity to them. People are often blinded by their own privilege, and scope the paper every morning on the way to work, or scroll through Twitter whilst having a cigarette, and gravitate towards the issues that they think could impact them or someone in their immediate circle most quickly. Often, when you are part of a marginalized community, this isn't a bad thing. As trans people, we are often constantly looking out for trans and non-binary people because we are nestled so tightly within our community, and our newsfeeds become flooded with transness all of the time, allowing us to feel integrated, aware, and part of our community's struggles and burdens but also our joy and our success.

But when decisions are being made by the most privileged – white cis men – looking at their newsfeeds and deciding what to care about, the self-serving nature of their care and their empathy often just fuels their own privilege in a way that doesn't leave any more drops of empathy for other people. All of their care and energy goes into their own kind, but unlike when that happens with the trans community, their power and dominance has structural impact, often wider than they even realize. As their privilege and strength continues, it ripples outward, crashing over marginalized groups, drowning them in waves of gender pay gaps, manspreading, turned down jobs and catcalling.

The nuance of identity is something that I want you to

remember. Something that is often lost when we see headlines about huge groups of people. Something that is so integral to us as a community that its importance is so much greater than we all even know. Identity is so talented and clever. It's something that can equally bring a community together, allowing us to all feel a part of the same group, whilst also individually giving each person their own different coloured light. It allows us to glow, and brighten the world, whilst ensuring that each of us shines in our own unique way. Kind of like when I went to see One Direction at The O2. A mass of people, all carrying a light, but this time, each light is their own.

Trans and non-binary people are often told that their lived experiences are this or that. Black or white. Male or female. There's no nuance in media depictions of our community. Often non-binary people like myself are lost within the discussion. It's either trans women or trans men. No room at the inn for non-binary people. The same thing often happens when we discuss LGBTQ+ rights. Often we hear some of the world's most prominent speakers discussing LGBTQ+ rights, and find ourselves waiting for our identities to be recognized. It's almost like queer bingo, or like waiting for at least one woman to be read out in the list of nominees for Best Director at the Oscars.

'*Two men, or two women, should be able to walk down the road and be able to hold each other's hands without prejudice. It's 2020; we should be able to do that,*' people say.

Of course, this should be true. There's power in being unapologetically queer, especially when that's being shared with someone else whom you love. But I can't help but wonder if (I can't promise that that's the only Carrie Bradshaw 'wonder' you will get in this book), and often feel that, there are issues that carry more urgency to them.

Honestly, I always have a twinge of guilt when I feel that, because what I want to actually say is: '*Hello, yes, I do understand this is not okay, and obviously something that we should all be able to do, but what about the fact that some people in this country literally don't think trans people should be able to exist, work, live, be educated or just like literally do anything because they're trans? What about the people across the world that are being murdered because they're trans? What about the fact that right now, trans suicide is on the rise, and nearly half of all trans people have attempted suicide?*'

But I don't. I sit back at the Pride event that I'm at, and I swig my wine, pop outside for a cigarette, and then put it on my close friends Instagram story.

I've got to a point now where I am tired. Twenty-two and tired. (That's what the next book's called.) Non-binary people are truly some of the most beautiful, cherished and delightful people that I have ever met. They're also some of the most boring; but that's fine, not everyone is perfect. We are some of the most intelligent yet frustratingly resilient people out there, and the magnitude of our minds both pains me and fills me with awe. For centuries we have existed, constantly knowing our truth and our validity. Knowing that we are wonderful. Knowing that although the world can't seem to place us anywhere, we have found our home and our space within each other. But often we are torn down so quickly that that joy is forgotten. Even though we know how special and how valid we are, the powers that be claw at our very being, making us feel like we are constantly being stripped of our essence. Stripped, and put back together in an easily digestible manner. Put back together so that we feel like we fit, even when we don't.

The landscape is torn. It's broken. Actually no, it's not broken, because the protections and provisions we need never existed to be broken. Non-binary and gender non-conforming identities have been continually erased from legislation, governmental forms and data-finding resources, and the fight for our identities to even be seen, let alone for institutions to change so they're accessible, is something we are within right now. In 2019 I campaigned for X passports in the UK, along with life-long campaigner Christie Elan-Cane, and now the fight continues with campaigners aiming to allow people outside of the binary to be able to identify as such on the 2021 census – a fact-finding and data-driven resource sent to every single person in the UK to find out more about how our own Government can do better. The current socio-political climate, exacerbated by the media's addiction to falsifying our existence, has meant that being trans/non-binary/gender non-conforming in the twenty-first century feels like constantly trying to prove your existence, despite our rich history that shows we've been here forever. The changes we are asking to be implemented aren't born out of newness, but from tiredness. They're long overdue. It leaves us feeling like we can't be placed anywhere, hence why our inter-community strength is so powerful and important to us. When we have to venture into the world, where we aren't heard, or listened to, it can feel like we are shouting against the wind. But if we all shout together, hopefully we will be heard. Hopefully, things will change.

The stories in this book are mine. They're my trials and tribulations, my mistakes, my successes, my terrors and my joys. My men that I've shagged, my clothes that I've worn. The times I have been able to see the wood through the trees, as well as the times when I've wanted the woods to bury me and for me never to see the light again. The mishaps when dating, the faux pas with fashion, my ridiculous, and still to this day, confusing path of life. But what I most want is for you to realize that this is *my* path. It's my way in this world. There is no one way to be non-binary, and truthfully that's one of the best things about it. It's an identity that is yours to shape, and create, and evolve. While I'm not a fan of Pokémon, this is what I imagine it to be like.

This has truly been one of the most fulfilling yet terrifying and nauseating experiences of my life: putting pen to paper to share parts of my life that even I wasn't aware of. My feet have walked a fair way, but others have walked longer, and harder, through tougher terrain. If anything, place yourself in our footprints, and resonate with them. Feel the warmth that they have left. Feel the energy that they expel. My story is a story that is full of ups and downs, but also privilege and awareness. Take yourself out of your own being and think, just for a second, of the lives of trans people, and how you can become a better person by helping us out. It doesn't seem like a lot to ask, truly. That warmth that comes from stepping in our footprints is a warmth of humanity and kindness. Putting yourself in our shoes should command you to do something for us, rather than question why we left those footprints in the first place.

As a community, our joy and our happiness are things that keep us going, and allow us to continue in a world that is constantly trying to push us out. Rejoice in our happiness, but listen to our hardship. We are more than what pushes us down. Take in our light, and allow it to brighten your mind.

The Key in the Lock

They were a pair of red suede boots with literally a slither of a heel, but they were enough for me to sit on eBay for two hours debating whether or not they would actually be worth it. Worth the aggravation. Worth the drama. Because I'm a huge queer cliché, I was obviously sat in bed, under my duvet as if I was watching the most explicit porn you could imagine, when in actual fact I was debating whether or not to go red or blue suede on the first of many boots that would grace my feet over the next five years. I decided to buy them. I decided there was no way that I wasn't going to have them. Even though they would probably cause a ruckus at sixth form. And who knew what would happen to the suede in the rain. It didn't bear thinking about. But, I needed them. That experience pretty much embodies the way in which I see fashion. In the most stubborn way possible, if I want it, and I think it's going to look cute, I will wear it and adorn it upon my body, rendering me bankrupt but stunning. It's not always been easy to make the fashion choices that I truly wanted, and it definitely wasn't an overnight change, but that night under my duvet was a turning point.

Gender expression is something that is not often spoken about when it comes to gender identity. Gender identity is the way in which you choose to self-identify your own gender. It's what you feel inside, and identifies the way in which you choose to exist within the world that we are all living in. Gender expression is simply the way that you decide to express that identity. So for cisgender people, traditionally, their gender identity would be either male or female, and they would express that gender in ways that are traditionally noted. Men in suits. Women in heels. Men in cargo shorts. Women in short shorts. But your gender expression can be literally whatever you decide it to be. For example, cisgender men whose gender identity is cis male can express their gender in an overtly feminine way, but still identify as male. Same goes for cis women. You can identify as a woman but express your gender in a way that is seen as traditionally masculine, and the expression doesn't negate the way in which you self-identify.

For me, that's the beauty of gender right there. Being non-binary, for me, means that there is no one way that I should look. Many people think that if you're non-binary, you have to express your gender in an androgynous manner. However, that's simply not true, because your gender expression is limitless. There is no set way any of us should look. There's no way that any gender should look, but the binary way in which people gender themselves comes with societal pressure to conform to traditional expressions of looking one way or another. Although it's completely valid for cis people to express their gender however they see fit, for me and many non-binary people, identifying as non-binary means that all of the arbitrary rules of how we should look just don't exist anymore. Freedom. Gender freedom. Fashion freedom.

My gender expression had always been feminine, even before I came out as non-binary. I always loved the elegance and drama of femininity. It was just so beautiful to me. I always used to think about how, when I was going out to dinner or somewhere fancy, it was infuriating that I was expected to take ten minutes to get ready. I was expected to throw on some fancy trousers and a shirt and tie, and then just be ready. I wanted to be able to take my time and have that moment of feminine elegance. When I was fourteen or fifteen, I used to always think, 'God, why can't I wear a ball gown to this family meal that's just going to be at Pizza Express?' Seeing pop stars and film stars all glammed up on the TV made me resent the fact that I wasn't allowed to do that. It just never sat right with me. Why wasn't I allowed? Who was telling me I couldn't?

Visibility for me is something that I now realize to be incredibly important but as only step one on the way to inclusivity and acceptance. It isn't as clear-cut and overtly positive as it sounds. Currently, as someone who works within the media and as a model, visibility is often something that I have to handle very carefully. Not because I have delusions of grandeur and think that I am truly the reincarnation of Princess Diana, but because of the ways in which it puts the spotlight on me and also on the non-binary community at large. It allows us to be visible in spaces where we truly aren't, which is beautiful. For example, the fashion industry is a place that has, over the past few years, showed prowess when it comes to trans and non-binary visibility and representation. Designers such as Gypsy Sport, The Blonds, Charles Jeffrey, Art School London and Opening Ceremony have championed LGBTQ+ people not just in their designs but in talent behind the scenes during the whole process. The creativity that brands like these have is a shining example of how visibility and representation matters by putting queer people in the body of the process, not just on the catwalk.

★

I became transfixed by the '80s. There was something about the concept of a huge shoulder span and a ridiculously snatched waist that was as appealing as it was terrifying: not just for my waist but for what this new exploration would mean for my fashion future. I knew from the second that I had seen these garments I needed them all over my body, and fortunately for me, a new vintage shop had just opened in my town. I popped in one day on my way home from sixth form and my world was transformed in the most clichéd way ever. The decadence of these garments that I had seen only online but were now in front of my little gay eyes was too much to handle. That, combined with the fact that I used to earn £10 a week from a paper round, meant that I was also unable to afford the visions that stood before me.

But in a surprise twist, what actually became the best part of my frequent trips to the vintage store wasn't just the hours spent trying on blouses and strutting around upstairs alone, it was the company in there. The two women who ran the shop were the first people to really just allow me to thrive when it came to fashion. I don't think at the time they realized they were doing anything, and to be quite honest it's only now as I look back on it that I realize how much they did for me at that time. It was freeing to just flick through the racks and revel in the artistry of the clothing, but also not to face judgement or drama for popping into the makeshift changing room and try on an '80s frock.

For many trans and non-binary people, we have that element of shame when it comes to expressing ourselves in ways that aren't deemed 'traditional'. Putting on that first pair of heels comes with a huge internal struggle. We have been socialized into a society that deems femininity weak, or wrong, and when that femininity is being portrayed through the body of a trans person, that shame and confusion as to whether or not this is 'okay' is all encompassing. The trying on clothes in secret. The trying on the lipstick in the bathroom when everyone is out. The trotting around in heels whilst no one is home, only to hear the key in the door and flick off that stiletto faster than Karren Brady on her way home from the boardroom. It's all done under the cloak of darkness. I understand that, and there's nothing wrong with that. The world is still a scary place for people who want to express their gender in ways that defy convention, especially femme identities, and specifically for people of colour.

But no matter where and no matter how, I think it's incredibly important that if our surroundings are preventing us from being able to explore our gender identity, or expression, that we try to find a space that allows us to investigate that part of ourselves fully. Our expression is so crucial, because allowing that side of us to breathe and feel nurtured is one of the finest acts of self-care and self-progression. It's about ensuring that we are able to do this in ways that feel safe and comfortable, and that's why I had so much freedom at the vintage shop. It was a place where I was able to just try on clothes that made me happy, in a space that was mine (however, I do remember that often people from sixth form would come in and I would hide in the changing room in my shell suits in fear of being spotted, but that's fine).

From that vintage shop I remember buying a black, faux-fur, long-line, vintage coat that at the time fell to the back of my knees. It was an oversized, silky-looking number, with the fur glistening and the collar excessively large. Lapels on lapels. I deemed it to be worthy of an actual purchase, rather than just a parade around the shop floor, as it was black and fairly unassuming and I thought it would be sixth form appropriate. I took her to the till, bobbed her in my bag and off we went.

As I was walking home, I decided that I was going to bite the bullet and just walk through the door in my new coat. 'What's the harm?' I thought. 'It's only a new coat.' I felt like my parents wouldn't even be that bothered, and would be more mindful of how much money I was spending rather than the fact that I was turning into a much younger but not quite as beautiful Joan Collins. I walked in and was greeted by compliments, which was a plot twist. I'd not expected an egging, but also didn't expect a full round of applause as if I was just coming off stage at the Palladium, so this reaction was actually succinct and pleasurable. I trotted upstairs and hung her up, ready for her first full day at sixth form the next day. I decided to wear her with a tie-dye button-up shirt and a pair of denim shorts that I had decided were too long so had rolled them up far enough that my pins were on full display. My new suede boots had arrived, and after swiftly running them upstairs in the dead of night, I planned my first ever full look. It's a far cry from the utterly earth-shatteringly beautiful looks that I pull now; however, at the time this was a moment. I felt fine about it for sixth form. I'd worn the shorts before, and people knew that I wasn't afraid of a print, so this didn't seem like it was going to cause too much of a commotion.

The coat was the talking point of the common room (for anyone who doesn't know, a common room is like a festering pot for sixth formers when they either have a free period, lunch, or decide they just want to lie down on the floor or snog their partner for far too long). I walked in and my group of friends couldn't look away. I was a weird pet to them for the day. Stroking, grabbing, gasping, it was all going wrong. The plan had taken an odd turn. I never wanted to be the centre of attention, but just to be able to wear this gorgeous full look, and go about my day like any other student. I was never popular at school and had a very close-knit group of friends of about three people. What was bizarre about this friendship group is that they were part of a wider group, which meant that from the outside looking in it might have appeared that I was popular; however, from the inside I can assure you that this wasn't the case. However, this intense dynamic meant that whenever I would go and sit with my friends in a free period or at lunch, I would mince over to this rather large group of about four girls and 289,180 guys. It was vile. They were vile. Obviously I was in love with one of them and fancied about three others, but that's fine. They didn't need to know that for the time being. When I went

27

over on that first day when I was wearing my full look, the boys erupted with laughter. I was unsure why, as this faux fur was absolutely delightful and in the least bit a stand-up comedian, but I ignored, flicked my fringe and gracefully sat down with my Nature Valley bar.

'Didn't realize Jamie was a pimp nowadays?' screamed one of them, their words flying over from their circle where the group were playing pool.

'Are you naked under there Jamie?' shrieked another. (I then realized that the coat was actually longer than my shorts, hence the comment about the nudity.)

The comments came thick and fast throughout the rest of the day, and people began to laugh and cackle whenever I would grace a hallway or a classroom. I was distraught. I didn't really know what to do or how to feel because I had felt such elation at how beautiful the coat was when I tried it on in the vintage shop and when I had seen it hanging in my wardrobe the night before, ready for its first outing. How was it that my relationship to this coat had changed so dramatically in such a short space of time? This was the first time that I would experience this constricting feeling. The feeling of being elated and yet terrified all at the same time. Of people pulling each thread of your joy, watching it unravel in their hands. A feeling that would follow me right up until this present day. A feeling that wasn't mine to feel. A feeling that shouldn't be mine to feel, and that was the most upsetting thing about it. That it was completely not my fault. But for me, that was a turning point in terms of fashion. I knew from that moment onwards that the way that I wanted to dress gave me so much more life and energy than the comments that it garnered.

Over the next two years I would create a wardrobe that was more me than it had ever felt before. I moved on from the impromptu fashion shows in the changing rooms at the tiny vintage store in town and allowed myself to wear these clothes in my bedroom and plan the barrage of looks that would grace the hallways from that moment on. It didn't feel like a choice at that moment. It wasn't a choice. It was a place that felt so comfortable, and I was so confused and hurt at how people were reacting because of the pure joy that it brought me. What was I doing wrong? So many of us feel this way and we need to remember that we are doing nothing wrong. Wearing clothes that make you feel happy and confident is never an act that we should feel ashamed about, nor is it an act we are doing for other people. I've never understood that notion, of wearing something for someone else's validation. I guess maybe two per cent of the reason we like to look nice is because other people might also think we look okay, but it was never the motivating factor in my spending my hard-earned money. It was more than that. It was an act of self-care and self-love, and being selfish in these instances is absolutely valid. Take your time, and find your footing with it.

I get asked a lot about how to get to a stage where you can just wear whatever you want and feel confident and happy in it. I always say to take your time. I think often our natural instinct is to rush, for many reasons. The first being that we know how elegant and beautiful and strong we are going to feel when we are wearing these clothes. The second is the fact that social media has meant we have role models and figures in our lives now that are just doing these amazing things, like wearing nine-inch heels to a meeting about taxes, or just wearing a dress and a casual lip to brunch. But what happens when we see these people is that we don't always see the story and the time that it takes to get to that point. For many of us it's not a quick fix, and that's okay. Allow yourself to take time and try things on with people that you feel comfortable with or by yourself in a little shop that makes you feel safe. It's a privileged statement to say, 'JUST WEAR IT' or 'JUST DO IT' because that doesn't take into account so many factors in our lives that can prevent us from doing so: our families, whether or not we are out yet publicly, whether or not we are in an environment where is actually safe to express ourselves and for us to wear what we want to wear. But what I will say is, no matter how hard you think it might be, or how isolated you might feel, there will always be a way that you can do it, and people that you can do it with. You can be free to express yourself. It will happen. No matter how long it takes, you will get there and you will be able to live aesthetically however you choose to. It's not always going to be easy, but you're going to be able to do it. Have a strong network of queer people and allies around you, if possible, and just revel in your own gender euphoria, because your body and your presence in this world should never be limited or shrunk due to fear.

After studying fashion for what felt like a literal eternity, I grasped an insight into the industry that really highlighted the work that needs to be accomplished within this environment. Yes, I know it's shocking, but I do in fact have a first class honours degree in Fashion Management and Marketing from the University for the Creative Arts Epsom, so Fashion Business is my card to play. It's essentially learning about sociology and fashion all in one. So this gave me a really interesting and unique insight into the ways in which the fashion industry works. Forecasting trends and looking at the ways social movements take over the creative industries, and how they feed into each other, was something that truly blew my mind. Specifically, I was fascinated by the ways in which gender was seen in fashion. When I started my studies, gender neutrality was a 'hot topic', or what the media described as 'The Trans Tipping Point'. We were in a time when gender was a discussion that had moved from an academic space into an environment that seemed bizarre yet thrilling. Fashion houses had begun to tackle the outdated movements of their own industry, with one of their first big moves being the merging of their menswear and womenswear shows into one big, hilarious strut-athon. This meant that menswear and womenswear were no longer separated when it came to consumers engaging with the collections, and it also implied that menswear and wom-enswear garments that were traditionally worn by either 'men' or 'women' no longer provided stereotypes that these brands wanted to pander to.

However, what it actually showed is that often the motivation behind gender neutrality, or 'merging' when it comes to gender and fashion, is not always coming from the heart, or even from a space of inclusion. Designers and fashion houses are businesses that are always looking to do what's best for their brand, and merging shows has many financial and logistical benefits. For example, putting on two shows a year that are mixed, rather than two womenswear and two menswear shows, means that the brand is saving money on show time, and also not having to produce as many garments as they normally would if they were showcasing a pure womenswear or pure menswear show. It is also something that often is used as a PR stunt. When the news came that brands such as Gucci were merging their menswear and womenswear shows into one big blob of overpriced delight, it gained a lot of press, and a mass fashionista discussion ensued. Why were they doing it? Was this a good idea? Would everybody now do this? And lo and behold, other large houses followed suit. But, as is so common with the fashion industry, when it came to male models walking the runway in what would be considered traditional 'womenswear' garments, it just didn't happen. High-fashion femininity was still monopolized by white cis women, whereas masculinity was something everyone was allowed to step into.

The struggles with fashion have always been there, and this comes from internalized transphobia and also internalized misogyny. Often for myself I would feel that I didn't want to appear 'too trans' or 'too femme' or 'too overt', as I didn't want to exude a level of confidence that felt threatening. Years of this thought process led me to a fashion revolution in 2018. Up to that point, I'd worn what I wanted and was so happy with the ways in which I expressed myself; however, something came around that I hadn't expected to throw that all off kilter. Summer. She arrived in late May/ early June and I was shook. I didn't know how to deal with her properly. It had been my first year at university and my fashion had taken off, due both to my new surroundings and to the plethora of vintage shops at my disposal. As soon as it started to get hot, I didn't know how to deal with the changes in wardrobe that this would mean for me. What it actually boiled down to was the fact that I'd wanted to wear skirts and dresses for a long time, but the internalized transphobia and fear was too much for me to be able to do so openly. But I knew at this moment that I couldn't supress this urge anymore. I'd worked so hard on my identity in those past few months after coming out as non-binary that I knew this was something that I just needed to do. I couldn't spend the whole summer a) too hot to breathe and also b) in looks that I didn't feel fully comfortable in. Here's that younger Jamie stubbornness coming into play again. Once I'd set my mind to something, I just knew I had to do it. It was the black coat all over again.

To test the waters I decided to go out for dinner, and to this very casual dinner I would wear a little velvet tube skirt. Nothing too ostentatious, but something I felt proud to wear.

I threw it on and immediately pulled it down so that it was at my knees. Not only did I look like a librarian, I also felt like I was giving in to the side of me that was telling me not to wear it. That it was too much. That this whole thing was just a bit silly. So in classic me style, I decided to pull it up so it was at the thigh. Sultry enough for me, and also suitable enough still for Pizza Express at 7 p.m. in central Surrey. I was bloody nervous, and much like most of the things that I deal with as a result of being non-binary, I didn't really tell anyone how I was feeling. I just decided that I was going to wear this skirt and just rock and roll. Much like the fur coat of yesteryear, I knew that it was going to cause a reaction. I knew that the looks would increase and the drama would reach simmering point, and that annoyed me. But the joy was too exponential for me to care. I was sixteen again, in that bloody coat, truly euphoric at how it was making me feel.

From that moment with the fur coat, to this moment with the velvet skirt, I felt a sense of achievement and also a really dramatic and over-the-top sense of emotion. I'd done it. I'd achieved what I'd wanted to do for so so long, and nothing horrendous had happened. I managed to eat a full margherita, not spill anything, and also enjoy the luxury of elasticated fashion, all in one evening. Iconic. And what's really great about moments like this for us is that then when we decide to do it again, and wear that skirt or that shirt or that suit out, it becomes less and less of an issue for us. We get less stressed. We feel less terror, and it becomes normalized in our wardrobe, as it should have always been.

Sadly, however, what this normalization and ease does is act as a stark reminder that we are not safe when we do then encounter harassment or public prejudice because of our fashion. Once I'd lost my skirt virginity, I relaxed into a state of comfort. The floodgates of ASOS opened, and I felt comfortable wearing clothes that I truly wanted to. But I was new to this charged anger that people I'd never met were now directing right at me. For other, narrow-minded people, we are a beacon to channel their hatred at. We are a target for their words and their violence. And that's important to remember: that it's theirs. Their words. Their anger. Their violence. Although it hits us, and hurts us, it's their words. They don't speak for us, and they never will. Our strength and our beauty in appearing gender non-conforming is what speaks volumes. It can have us running to the toilets and taking it all off and running home because the world isn't ready for the power that non-binary and gender non-conforming people have. But what we won't do is forget that power. Fashion and beauty have power. No longer are we covering up. We are adorning our bodies with fashions that bring our identity to the surface. Unapologetically dressing yourself so that you feel comfortable and excellent is truly one of the best forms of self-care that we can do. Whether that be a plain T-shirt and khaki shorts, or a full-on ball gown and stilettos, it doesn't matter where you're going: there are no rules or limits to the excellence that gender non-conforming people can exude.

2 THINGS TO THINK ABOUT WHEN EXPLORING FASHION

1. There are no rules. There are no times when you should or shouldn't wear something; that is all a literal lie tied into patriarchy and misogyny, to silence trans bodies. Don't listen to people who tell you that you should wear certain clothing for certain occasions. Job interview? Wear the ball gown. Nipping to get some milk and emergency Lemsip because you've started to get a runny nose? Wear a suit. Do whatever makes you happy with fashion.

2. Take your time, especially when it comes to being you in public. Know that this isn't a failure, and that you're allowed to be as masc/femme as you desire, but that it's a journey. Taking your time doesn't negate the fact that you're going to get there; it just means you're sadly having to be practical about the world and climate that we are living in.

My relationship with fashion has now evolved into something that is monumental. I still get as excited when I find a new coat or a new pair of heels as I did when I used to strut around the little vintage shop at home, because I have learnt to appreciate the joy that fashion gives me. I've learnt and cherished the way in which fashion is an extension of myself, rather than something that hides or covers me. It's an illusion. A tool that makes me feel like I am truly here. The reaction to which is a part of my life that still causes me pain, that I can't control, but that is drowned out often by the inner joy of knowing how proud sixteen-year-old Jamie would've been. Like the journey with our identity, our journey with our bodies and the way we look is something that often only realizes its true potential when we are retrospective. Allow yourself to remember how far you've come. Now, literally no clothing is off-limits. Looking back, I would never have thought I'd be able to wear some of the pieces of clothing I've worn in the past two years. For me, this progress isn't just motivated by aesthetic. It's a progress that has allowed me to love being non-binary and love myself for figuring out the intricacies of my own identity. Fashion was the key that unlocked the possibilities of feeling joy.

Hydrangea Bush

I've never written about my family before, but I guess that might be for two reasons. The first being they all love beige and are ardent wearers of flat shoes, which truly is uninspiring aesthetically. It can be very firmly said that if my family tree were real and growing somewhere in an orchard, I'd be that random hydrangea bush growing just out of the way but still in sight; you don't really know how it got there, but it's growing and actually adds a generous splash of colour and hilarity to the picture. The second reason is that I am privileged to have a family that aren't the archetype of many tales of families when it comes to queerness. There are elements of my familial experience that do fit that narrative;

however, in short, my family are fairly Switzerland. They're supportive yet hesitant. Knowing yet unknowing. Aware of the crust, but not the centre. Kind of like a Camembert.

For those of us fortunate enough to have good relationships with our families, I wonder if the still-mild strain or distance in the relationship is often because of things that aren't identity specific. Maybe they're universal challenges that all twenty-somethings face with their parents. Being in your twenties and having parents, I've decided, is weird. As many of us wade through our twenties, we are grasping at notions of actually having some form of adult life. It's that terrifying feeling of actually doing it on your own. Doing your own food shops. Looking after your own finances (if possible), catching your own spiders. But is it just because we are growing autonomous in our lives as human beings that a potential divide is created or there is a 'lack of closeness' within a family unit, or is it the queerness? Or is it both? Is queerness the catalyst to the already pre-existing separation that occurs with some millennials and their families?

There's a history of queerness being synonymous with fraught and fractured family relationships, and I think, much like a lot of prejudice that is targeted towards the LGBTQ+ community nowadays, many people believe that this family tension is now a thing of the past. They think that young queer and trans people being thrown out of their houses for being LGBTQ+ is no longer a reality. Yet it's still happening. Not just across the UK, but around the world. In the UK, 24 per cent of respondents to the Government's 2017 National LGBT Survey shared that they weren't open at all with any members of their family about being LGBTQ+. In a surprising twist, younger people were more likely to keep their identity to themselves, with 42 per cent of cisgender 16–17-year-olds also not open to any members of their family about their identity. That's a staggeringly high statistic: nearly half of 16–17-year-olds who identify as cisgender, but not heterosexual, were not comfortable being 'out' to their families due to fear of what they would say or rejection.

These statistics do fall short of exploring the numbers for trans individuals, and specifically non-binary people. However, what was an interesting find was that a higher percentage of respondents to the survey who were under 35 identified as non-binary compared with those who were older. Fifty-seven per cent of those under the age of 35, so essentially the sexy millennials, identified as non-binary compared with 36 per cent of the over 35s (God, this is like *The X Factor*). Critics discussed that this was because non-binary was a 'new term', and tried to correlate it to a trend in 'gender non-conformity', but history will continue to prove that that is just not the case. What it actually *is* is a trend in young people leading the investigation. It's a trend in changing your own narrative, using knowledge, tools and information that are centuries old. Ensuring that we don't allow the status quo to wash over us and set us in stone. They're stripping away the conditioning that we are all subject to because of western colonialism and the influence of the gender binaries on how we are raised, educated and seen. Quite rightly so. Much like party politics, the generational divide means that younger people are more often than not open to exploring structures that they're told are the norm in order to see whether or not they actually are.

Most media depictions of trans people in family situations are ones of turmoil and confusion. Come to think of it, I've never seen trans people the focus of any campaign, or media-fronting imagery that has trans people within the family unit simply existing and being a family. There's always a spin on it that something is wrong. Always highlighting a trans-shaped problem somewhere in the family mechanism.

One major example of this was the programme *Butterfly*, which aired on ITV in 2018. It was the story of a 'traditional family unit' with a child named Max who was trans. Although the story and depiction of many of the events in Max's life were realistic – in part due to the fact that trans charity Mermaids had helped and supported the show's writing and production process – I was still left feeling frustrated. The whole series was centred around the dialogue between the parents: how Max being trans affected them, how it impacted the other children in the family. Why are we, as trans people, and even more specifically as non-binary people, not allowed to see the family unit as something that is just able to be, without cataclysmic implosion? It ended with Maxine's mother, played by Anna Friel, escaping abroad with Max to find hormone blockers for Maxine due to the long waiting times in the UK. Although dramatized, this is a genuine occurrence for many families at the moment. A situation where many parents want to do right by their child, but they themselves are in unknown waters. They're running off of political and social commentary on trans young people in the back of their minds as they decide what's right for their children.

But like most things, the most important thing to do here is just listen to the young person. Only they know in this instance what it's like to be young, trans and amongst a family of people that are so often all cis. I think there's something, potentially, about British culture that doesn't allow young people to have views that are able to be legit-imized. We are seen as people that are too experimental or fragile to actually form our own views and identities, and constantly have to have an adult's 'approval' of whatever we are thinking or feeling. Although there are many families up and down the country and across the world that think having a trans child is the worst thing possible a lot of families simply end up not knowing where to turn or what to do when they find out that their child is trans. Many look to the Gender Identity Development Service (GIDS) or Gender Identity Clinics (GIC) for guidance as to what to do; however, the waiting times, which are approximately eighteen months to two years, mean that they often end up going private, or putting off their child's transition because the delay is outwith their control. But through all of this hustle and bustle and back and forth is a young trans person just wanting to exist as themselves. To be able to thrive in a body, a mind, a skin that they feel like they are able to stretch and move within. That is the most important thing to remember here. It's not about you, it's about them.

For me, the relationship that I have with my family is often preceded by the childhood notion of acceptance. We are socialized to believe that we need our family's full approval and acceptance to be able to feel content with how we exist. And even if that acceptance is 80 per cent achieved, there's still that 20 per cent in flux, making you feel like your identity isn't as secure as you'd hoped it to be or feel. Whether you have your parents' full support or not, one thing needs to remain constant, and that is that your identity is valid. Your parents' and family's approval shouldn't change who you are, and if you don't have that support there, know that you are able to forge and create your own chosen family within the LGBTQ+ community. We are here for you. Despite our differing lived experiences, many of us are here for you in all of the ways that your family may not be, because we know what that feels like. Only now have I been able to realize that, and essentially dismantle and disregard this notion that we need a metaphorical thumbs-up from our parents on all aspects of our lives.

My experiences of being the only out queer person amongst a fairly traditional family unit have been fairly anti-climactic, which for me and many others is often the best-case scenario and a privileged position to exist within. Growing up, there were never any rampant discussions of homophobia or transphobia; however, that still didn't stop me from feeling terrified of coming out. Often with LGBTQ+ people, even if there are no warning signs of queer-phobic behaviour or language amongst our family, we are still bombarded with the narrative that coming out is either going to be absolutely ideal and no drama, or it'll be the end of your relationship with your family as you know it. There's no in-between. However, in reality that's not always the case. For me it definitely wasn't. What stopped me was the innate fear that the latter would occur. Even though there was no evidence that would be the case, as human beings we often focus on what the worst outcome could be so that if that does happen, at least we are prepared. If anything else marginally better than that happens, it's a triumph. Interestingly I never actually had that euphoric, dramatized 'coming out' that many queer people seem to have. I've never sat down with any member of my family and had the quivering-lip chat. I think a large part of me knew that they knew, and although it's powerful to sit down and come out on your own terms and actually be vocal and proud of your identity, I never really felt like that was something I wanted to partake in. It all seemed a bit dramatic for my liking, and also meant that I would have to be incredibly emotionally vulnerable with people that I'd known all my life, which even now I find a daunting task. Much easier to be emotionally vulnerable with strangers. Duh.

Coming out was something that was done *for* me during school and throughout sixth form. I wasn't allowed to come out on my own terms, and my body, presence, voice, everything was a sign for other people to continually tell me what I was from as early as the age of ten. Although it was true, I didn't have the autonomy of that part of my existence, and that hurt. This trickled over to my family life too. Due to the fact that at school everyone just knew, and assumed I was gay, I never really felt like I had to come out at home because I presumed they would be thinking the same. This might sound like the best-case scenario, but it still meant there was a fairly large elephant in the room. Whenever we'd be watching *EastEnders* and there was the annual gay kiss, I'd turn to stone in my seat, not moving, knowing that whatever my reaction was would be a sign to them that I was in fact, le homosexual. What this did, though, was take a moment away from me. It took a moment where I would've been able to bond, share and be emotionally vulnerable with those nearest to me. Even to this day, I still struggle with sitting down with my family and saying how I am, or what I'm feeling, even though they continually tell me that I can do that. The repercussions of my childhood still snake their way into my everyday life over a decade later.

The same happened with coming out as non-binary. Unlike sexuality, I knew that this one was a little more complex. If coming out as gay was the technical challenge on *Bake Off*, coming out as non-binary was the showstopper. It was something that required practice but could end up with a soggy bottom (?). I knew that it needed to be something I couldn't 'presume' they knew, like the whole gay thing. It was something that required allyship, understanding and a conversation. However, that's not really my way of doing things. The idea of having to sit down with the four members of my close family and discussing being non-binary sounded positively revolting, so I decided to do what all millennials do and talk about it online first. Test the waters. Testing the waters online is a little different though. Online, we can cultivate our spaces to some extent, and on certain platforms; allow specific people to see just what we want, and vice versa. This meant that the people I was sharing my new shiny gender identity with were either part of the LGBTQ+ community or genuine allies that I knew would support me through and through. Despite the reaction online being positive, I knew the reaction closer to home could be completely different. A situation that I wasn't really ready for, so again, like most twenty-somethings, I decided to just not do it. It wasn't that I thought they'd abandon me, but I presumed they just wouldn't care. That they wouldn't understand, and instead of trying to, they would pretend none of it had happened.

At the time, I was eighteen and had all the arrogance that comes with being a new-born adult. I felt like they were a distant part of my life, and that they'd know when I wanted them to. I was going to live my somewhat secret, yet loud, bold and brash non-binary life in London without them knowing, and it was going to be brilliant. And it was. For a bit, it was brilliant. I felt the most free I'd ever felt in my life. But it was always in the back of my head that I would have to do this. A rattling in the back of my brain whenever anything good happened in my life, I would remember that all was not as well as I'd want it to be. Rather than doing it in person, sat on the end of my bed crying, I decided to share it very publicly online and allow my mother to see it. The time had come to unblock her and finally allow her to see the hilarious secret life I was living. She would then be able to make up her own mind, and I would find out through WhatsApp what her thoughts were.

It turned out that there was no backlash. Instead, what filled that gap was a borderline ignorance to the issue. Just as I had anticipated, there was a feeling of 'this isn't happening'. A feeling of, 'yes we see that you're living your life in this way, but we don't really get it so we're going to allow you to do so, but not really understand any part of it'. It wasn't spoken about for the first year or so. Although it was something that online I was constantly harping on about, when it came to travelling the two hours and forty-eight minutes home, upon arrival I was just white cis-gay Jamie. As if the life I had been living outside of Dorset wasn't actually something that was real or tangible. It felt like a bubble of joy that I had created since leaving home, and I worried that returning home could burst that.

It took years. Only now, as a twenty-two-year-old, three years later, am I able to say that they are in fact allies. Mum and my sister, Beth, more than anyone else, but the rest are no longer living under a blanket of complete ignorance (just maybe sometimes draping themselves with a blanket of it). A slight sliver of 'what are you on about?', but still at least trying to be there and understand. Pronouns are the last thing to come. For me, it's still a daily hiccup with them, but I know that they're trying. Pronouns are important, and to be misgendered will always feel like burning yourself with a pair of straighteners on your ear or using one of those hot taps that instantly goes scorching as soon as you put your palms underneath its stream. It's hard to hear it, but it comes with a suffix of 'we're trying'. A feeling of familial 'we'll get there, just give us time'. But when you live, socialize and exist amongst people outside of your family unit who don't have any qualms about using they/them pronouns, the frustration and pain seems legitimate when it for some reason takes members of your family years to do something that they already practise within their vernacular. It still makes me wonder if the inability to use the right pronouns means that somewhere, deep down, there's a slight harbouring of resentment and lack of care or belief for your identity. But with family, it's often a generational thing, as well as a time thing. Many of the people we're asking to change their language have been using other pronouns for you for decades, so asking them to change this overnight can be something that takes time. But what I have found helps is instead of correcting them every time they get it wrong, I now just don't answer. If someone asks me a question that includes a 'he', I don't respond. Partly to make a point, and partly because I forget that they're talking about me. They'll get there, but remember that when you are surrounded by your nearest and dearest and they're still not getting it, this is in no way an indication of your identity and its validity. You are as valid as you are when you're surrounded by your trans family; it's just that this one might take a little longer.

Moving away and being independent really helped. Not to say that I don't care about my family's progress and education anymore, but it puts into perspective the strength of family. Much like romantic relationships, I no longer place all of my happiness, strength and sense of approval in how my family treats me. I get that from myself and my queer family, which feels like a healthier and easier balance. Also in part, it's to protect myself from disappointment. Placing your validity and acceptance in any one group of people is something that often leads to disappointment. It's now evenly distributed across my family and my 2.5 friends, for my sake, and my sake only. (It also means that the potential disappointment you may feel when someone does slip up or becomes a bit of a dick is less impactful, and you can just gradually phase them out of your life. Brilliant.)

★

2015 was an interesting year. I had just turned eighteen and was about to begin my A levels. I'd chosen Seventeenth Century History, Food and Nutrition, Sociology and Biology (a real mix, and obviously food was my favourite. An A level in cooking! Sure!). In terms of my identity, at this point I was still identifying as a gay man; however, my fashion had taken an exquisite and flamboyant turn. Our sixth form was attached to our secondary school, so the transition was seamless, but the major difference was the ability to be allowed to wear your own clothes. A game changer for me. I was now able to experiment to my heart's content. This was really a time for me, as we previously discussed, where I was able to finally explore and see fashion as a vast sea of options, rather than a constricting uniform that I had to wear every day. The heels came out, the floor-length faux fur came, and the '80s flare began to flourish, much to the shock horror of many. But for me, it just felt right. I was able to do whatever I wanted to do and still be me at the same time. Just a taller and even more beautiful version.

Now for context, I have an interesting family set up. You know in *Love Island*, when two couples split up, and then one person from each couple ends up getting together? Well that's essentially what my parental situation is. My dad, Richard (or Dick when I want to wind him up), was with someone else, and had my half-sister Charlotte; and my mother, Claudia (like off of Winkleman), had two, creating George and Beth. They then created this unit of two people, who combined had three children from previous relationships. An amalgamation of human-sized baggage, to be frank. I then arose after they decided to create another child, therefore presenting me with one half-brother and two half-sisters. My dad's first child, Charlotte, was much older than me, and when I was born she was well into her teens. However, my mum's first children, George and Beth, were only a matter of digits older than me, so during my childhood I spent most of my time growing up with them.

We lived together and I essentially spent most of my life living in a two-parent, three-children household. Me, George and Beth. For a long time, I didn't actually realize that they weren't my 'full' siblings, but upon finding out, I didn't really care because the childhood and relationship that we'd had whilst growing up was very much that of a 'conventional family'. I know this family unit is fairly common, but when it comes to family tree shenanigans, I can only just understand that your mum's mum is your gran.

This meant that Charlotte, my older half-sister, wasn't as close to me during my childhood, teenage years and essentially all of my life. When I was a teenager, she was well into her twenties, so the difference in age was just too grand to form some kind of relationship. We ended up being just 'Christmas siblings', when we would just see each other once or twice a year.

What I find interesting is the notion of blood being thicker than water. This idea that because we are bound in some way by DNA our relationship is now necessary to exist in a stronger sense than our relationship with our friends, or anyone else for that matter. I understand it, obviously. With family that you're close with, there's an interesting bond that is actually very hard to describe. Even if you're not 'best friends' with some members of your family, there's a bond there: an invisible wire that tethers you all together in an orgy of cobweb genetics. A feeling of simply having history with this person, even if you can't vocalize it. But what I do find troubling about that notion, which many queer people also relate to, is that no matter your family members' opinions or thoughts, you have to continue that strong and resilient connection. Take '*that* uncle', for example. We somehow are told to 'forgive and forget' or allow the racism or xenophobia because he is 'your uncle' and 'he's old'. But that's never been something I could stomach. Definitely as I grew older, and realized that the energy we give to others when forging relationships is so precious and valuable, I came to the conclusion that there's truly no need to make effort with members of your family that aren't giving you the love, attention, care and support you need. This obviously isn't as black and white as not speaking to your handsy cousin at Christmas, as many people have this relationship with their mothers and fathers, and it can truly crush queer people and put them in vulnerable and insufferable positions. But I think it's still important to remember that wherever you are with your family there's always a plan B, and it's the LGBTQ+ community. We are your family. No blood is needed to cement you into the framework of the queer family tree, and even with its contentions and ups and downs, the notion of a 'chosen family' is something that, for many, is a lifeline. A hand to hold. A phone to ring when there's no one picking up elsewhere.

My siblings are all relatively similar, and I essentially slot onto the end. I guess visually it would be like if you were at a BBQ and there were vegetable kebab skewers, and then on the end of one there was just a chunk of pineapple. I am that pineapple. Not necessarily better than the rest of the kebab, but definitely sweeter, with some people thinking it's unnecessary. George and Beth both hilariously look the same, and when we all had our glasses on and used to take those awful family pictures together, we'd all look like different variations of the same human being. Nothing pleases me more than seeing families that all look the same; it's truly hilarious. You know when a family unit has one defining feature – a dimple, a bold eye or pointy ears – and everyone in the family Christmas card has the exact same features? Yeah, that's my favourite. They wouldn't mind me saying that they are fairly generic human beings. Common, if you will. White, straight, cisgender rural town folk who now have their own lives. We get on, don't get me wrong, but there's definitely a difference in our communication. As I've grown older, it's got better, and we now have an evolved and more mature connection, especially with Beth, but there's still a slight distance. Even though there are only a matter of years between us, the differences in social evolution and generational exploration that have occurred societally in the years that separate us has meant that Beth, who is seven years my senior, interacts and engages in the world in a very different way to me, a Gen Z masterpiece. My other half-sister, Charlotte is, to be honest, a person that I've not truly engaged with fully. It's an odd feeling to have a person who is a part of your family that you're not really that close with, or whose favourite colour you don't even know. There used to always be an urgent desire in my younger years to try and build a relationship with her that was the same as my relationship with George and Beth, but it never arose. Awaiting her arrival at Christmas was odd. It always felt like a very stylish stranger was just strolling in. But on the flip side, why would I have expected someone in their late twenties with their own life and job to come and pay attention to a thirteen-year-old ginger kid?

What is common amongst many trans people with not just members of their family but friends and co-workers is the silent discontent. It never surfaces as a face-to-face confrontation or verbal abuse per se, but it's there, underlying and bubbling under the surface of every conversation. A micro-aggression that actually is so piping hot and permanent that it turns into a boiling macro-problem very swiftly. It's the oppressor's, favourite tool, as if we were to bring it up and accuse them of it, we would be instantly gaslit with a barrage of 'When did I EVER say anything transphobic to you?' or 'I don't have a problem with you looking like this at all!'

This all came to a head in 2015, around our favourite hetero institution. A wedding. To this day I've still never actually been to a wedding; however, Beth has just got engaged to her what I would describe as 'normal hot' boyfriend Gary. (I know... It's hard to imagine a hot Gary but there's always Gary off of *Miranda* who was quite hot so...swings and roundabouts.)

It was a wedding I didn't even really care about. My mum's sister Sue was getting married, and this was a woman whom I'd met perhaps once when I was two, so my invitation seemed rather a formality than anything else. Despite this, I was ready. The looks were being planned, the drama was ready to be served and I was primed ready with my flowers in my basket, ready to take that one-two step down the aisle as designated flower girl/boy. I was eighteen, had just embarked on university and was really in the beginnings of exploring my gender identity in the most prominent way yet. I was feeling free, and to be honest, fairly invincible as I had managed to create a very close-knit, supportive group of people who were allies from the very beginning. One weekend I returned home, and my parents ominously tiptoed around me. I knew something was coming, and thought it was probably the fact that my bank statements were being sent to my home address and they'd seen how much money I'd been spending on pumpkin-spiced lattes and lipstick.

'*So... We need to talk to you about something*' is something you never want to hear from your parents. I was catapulted back to being ten and having them discover my dickpig-esque searches on Google and being told off for watching 'young twink gets double penetrated face fuck caught outside'. But no, this time it was something different.

'So Sue's wedding...she's sent out the invitations and you're invited!'

I mean, at this point I was shook that even the possibility of me *not* being invited was on the table so, straight off the bat, I wasn't impressed.

'But she's said that you can only come if you're wearing a suit. Sue doesn't want you to pull focus on the day and have all her friends and family asking about you as...you know... it's their wedding day.'

This notion that people being their authentic selves creates 'unnecessary' attention is one of the most frustrating conversations to try and have, because surprise, surprise, the unwanted 'unnecessary attention' usually comes from the very people complaining about it, rendering it in no way our fault. It's this idea that our whole narrative and identity is steeped in being an extrovert for extrovert's sake. This misconception that our whole presentation, our identity, our being, is some huge call for attention, and we just want to be seen as 'that' quirky, idiosyncratic person. A costume. A performance to attract eyes, rather than an expression that should attract allyship and support. I was baffled. This was the first time that I'd experienced genuine disapproval and prejudice from a member of my family, and even though we weren't close, it rippled through me. It forced my parents to have to have this conversation with me, which we know I am not a fan of. They were truly torn about what to do. As parents, most of the time they want to see a harmonious family unit come together, hence why they were trying to convince me to 'just for one day' do what my mother's sister had said so that we could just enjoy the wedding. 'Just don't be yourself for one day, and celebrate this repulsively heterosexual patriarchal institution, and then have a really basic vegetarian option at the dinner...just for one day!'

Bollocks to that.

As gender non-conforming people, we are often known

for being very stubborn and forthright, through years of experiencing people telling us we are 'too much' or 'not real' or 'PC culture gone mad'. I don't really enjoy this phrase, but we have a 'tough skin'. We experience walls, barriers and problems because of our gender identity, and that's often amplified by the other intersectional barriers that pile on top of that. It's a sad truth that many of us have been weathered so acidicly by the onslaught of transphobia and binary systems that exist within our society that we have become so eroded that we are numb to its impact. Our exterior is so worn that when issues like this arise in our lives, we are purely unsurprised. We then navigate through this problem like any other day, because sometimes that's just what it is. Another day. Another day of the same shit.

I stood my ground and told my parents that I wouldn't be attending the wedding unless I was allowed to go as my authentic self, wearing whatever I deemed comfortable, to celebrate their 'live laugh love' themed bash. (Which obviously would've been a white gown because I've heard through the grapevine that you're definitely allowed to wear those to weddings.)

Like many parents of non-binary children, it was new territory for my parents, and often this uncharted territory makes discussions like this hard. My parents eventually, after a long conversation that actually allowed us to talk about some of the realities of being a non-binary person in the twenty-first century, accepted my decision not to attend. I had guilt for causing this rift and for causing this issue, which is that internalized transphobia and misogyny that we all live with. Marginalized people often feel like their identity is the problem when it comes to family situations. We can feel like the burden. That if we weren't the way we were, this problem would never have surfaced. But that's exactly the point here. We are the way we are, and there's no way we can change that. There's not a single thing that needs to change from our end, on the way that we are existing within a society that is so binary and heteronormative that it's crushing us all. Asking us to push away the very walls that are constantly crushing us into small, confined boxes is toxic.

I didn't go to the wedding and I moved on with my life, with a heavy heart and a new sense of empathy for members of the trans and non-binary community that have it so much harder than me. This instance with my aunty was the tip of the iceberg of what goes on behind closed doors for so many non-binary people in their family units. I am blessed to have supportive parents. Even though they're still on that journey to allyship, it's a privilege to be able to acknowledge that they are even on it. That they've stepped aboard and are taking the journey alongside me. For that, I will forever be thankful. Cheers Dick and Clauds.

4 THINGS I WOULD SAY TO A NON-BINARY PERSON ABOUT NAVIGATING FAMILY

1. Although it might feel urgent, take your time when telling your family about who you are and your identity. Even if you have the most loving family in the world, sometimes it's better to ensure that you feel comfortable and sound enough in your own headspace and identity to share that with the world.

2. Know that you don't have to answer all their questions. They're going to have questions, because most families – unless they already have a member of the unit who identifies as non-binary – might not be familiar with the ways in which trans people need support. But this doesn't mean that you have to suddenly have non-binary as your specialist subject on *Mastermind*. Answer as much or as little as you see fit because it's not your job to be the constant educator of your nearest and dearest.

3. De-pedestal the notion that family are everything. Now this is a hard one, because we are socialized and

raised to see our families as the people that we have to hold closest to us and tell everything to at all times. But as non-binary people, often 'coming out' or sharing your identity with your family is not that simple. It's full of potent risk. It can truly endanger lives and risk the roof over your head, which is why finding a non-blood related but community-focused and concentrated family of non-binary and trans siblings is so important for our survival. De-pedestalling your family doesn't mean you don't love them, but it's ensuring that you don't look to your family as your one source of constant reassurance and support, because sadly often they're not.

4. Know that your relationship will grow. It will evolve and things will change. Be ready for that and find other resources of love and strength from within the community so that if things change for the worse, you will have a support system right behind you, all the way.

When you're in your twenties and you're beginning to forge a life for yourself, going back to the geographical location of your family relationships can feel like a regression. Visiting your family in your old home town and driving past the same old haunts where your childhood occurred and knowing that at one point in time, there was a younger you, a more vulnerable and fragile you, walking around these streets trying to figure things out, can be hard to relive. Even if it is ten years on. For me this really did impact the ways in which I saw the act of visiting home. I just wouldn't. Not because I didn't want to see my family, but because of the emotional labour of existing in a small town such as Dorchester.

Dorchester is the county town of Dorset, but don't get too excited: there's a van that drives around selling sandwiches that plays the ice cream van tune, foolishly tricking me and many young children that dairy was on its way when it was actually an egg mayo. There's an old Roman ruin that's particularly good to drive to at midnight and eat McDonald's in when you're seventeen and think that's an appropriate thing to do. It was a place of conformity. One of those small towns that was the archetype of Britain. If you were to show a New Yorker Dorchester and ask them where this was in the world, they'd instantly say the UK. It just was that type of place. One high street, two clothes shops, the same market every Wednesday, the same people having coffee in the same shops, every day, just bobbing about. It was a place that I genuinely loved, but also a place where I was fervently bullied, ridiculed and shamed for just existing. A place that I had formed a relationship with, but that relationship was turbulent and triggering. Moving away from Dorchester was one of the best things that ever happened to me, so returning always filled me with dread because it threw me straight back into the mindset of being the outcast that everybody knew. I remember being eighteen and people in their twenties telling me that going back home will change for you when you get older, and I never believed them. I never knew how I would get around this dichotomy of seeing my family while having to spend time in a town that hated me, but as I grew older and became more content with my life outside of Dorset, I realized that it was possible.

To be able to cherish the people in a place without giving power to the geographical location to allow your mind to revisit those traumatizing times is something I'm still to this day working on. But it's great to have a new-found relationship with not only my home town but my family. Looking at the whole package of your home town, with your family tucked away within it, in a new light as a different person, knowing that your relationship with your family is maturing as you mature, is equally as important. It allows you to realize that visiting your home and your family doesn't have to make you revert to being the younger version of you that might have found it difficult there, because although that was you, it's not you now. It will never be you again. It was you in a period of time that you've now moved on from, and it's an act of self-care and self-appreciation to allow yourself to move on from that. Not to forget it, because we never can, but to realize that it is in the past. Old. Done. It's shaped us into who we are now, and we owe it to ourselves to be able to move on so that we can continue to see our family and friends back home, so we can continue to build that relationship with them, whatever stage it's at.

If we are to take a look at non-binary as being about stripping away the restricting ideal that you have to be 'male' or 'female', we should also begin to apply that concept of fluidity to other aspects of our life, including our relationships with our friends and family. We don't need to see only people we have a blood relation to as our family. We can thrive and be strong without these bonds between us and our family. Tear up the idea of what it means to be a family, and realize that much like romantic love, it's not the relationship that should sit at the top of the pyramid. Forge relationships with queer people from your own community, your friends you have now, and the people you hold dear in person and online as your own, beautiful, queer and supportive family. Yes. this is sometimes easier said than done, but we all have at least one person that we can count on and cherish, so let's use that as the catalyst to create and hone our own bespoke, beautiful and strong family unit. Cherish the moments with your blood-related family, as it will change and evolve as you do. Things can get easier. Pronouns can become commonplace. But if that's not your reality, remember and know, deep in your heart, that it's possible to find the love and allyship in other queer and non-binary people that is so often missing from members of your family. So many of us wouldn't be here if that weren't true. We are all living proof of that.

SS Poly

In a world where we are rapidly finding our future part-
ners/future next shag online, dating has become a scene
that is full of complexity and carefully executed self-mar-
keting. From app to app, website to carefully selected online
group, we are dipping our toes into worlds that seem to offer
us an unknown amount of potential *potential*. Fortunately
this problem is something that, no matter what gender we
are, we who choose to date all face. Yes, there are specific
problems that trans and non-binary people face, but I think
something that binds us all is the whirlwind that is dating
in the twenty-first century. Its ups and its downs, its many
disappointments and let-downs. Its *'Oh I thought this was a*

date but it looks like you just want to shag – fine' moments. Its *'God I've only just met you but I literally think I love the shit out of you'* scenarios.

Like me, many queer people grew up in rural areas of the world where queerness and non-heterosexual relationships were not in abundance. We actively had to search them out. We were not surrounded by the gorgeousness of queer rela-tionships on our doorsteps, and not even necessarily on our TV screens or within our books. It was a constant mission to try to find that level of representation so that just for one second we could feel like we were actually capable of love and tenderness and companionship. Often we find our first glimpse of queer connection through sex, which can then tamper with our future view of what it means to be in a queer relationship. Is it all about sex? Or is it allowed to be more than that?

Fast forward to now and queer relationships in the media are more prominent. The Conservative Government are waving their pathetic rainbow flag and pedestalling themselves as 'gay icons' for legalizing same-sex marriage, which yes was amazing, but doesn't necessarily equate to a social change when it comes to the general viewpoint of same-sex marriage and relationships culturally. But what I'm more interested in is what's beyond same-sex relationships.

To so many people this notion of two cis men or two cis women being together was groundbreakingly edgy. It was something that they saw as a liberal mirage, something they'd only see on *Skins*, floating in the distance, or something that only happened in Brighton or the depths of Soho, when in actual fact it was happening right on their doorstep. But relationships are so much more interesting than that. The beauty of trans relationships is something we never see or hear about, and if we do, it's sensationalized into misleading headlines or inappropriate puns. We often find ourselves with a lot of love inside of us, and a yearning and want for companionship and care. And if the media coverage and general horror stories about trans people are anything to go by, we should be the group that needs that love and care more than ever. But the question here is, should that love and care always have to be supplied intravenously within a romantic relationship? Are there other ways we can receive that love without it having to be packaged into romance from just one other person?

Now, I wouldn't call myself a serial dater, but I do love the drama of throwing on an elegant dress and heels and going for dinner with an actual human being, rather than by myself with my laptop. There's something about going on a spontaneous date that makes me feel like I may or may not have my life together. It makes me feel very Kirstie Allsopp. Dating is something that we're taught is a rite of passage for all people. No matter who you are or what you're doing with your life, if you're not dating or seeing someone, there's a part of you that's incomplete. It's a message that is drilled into us from day one. We are born, and instantly when little baby boys have pictures with little baby girls, they're told they're going to be 'little heartbreakers'. When we're in school and everyone around us is getting into relationships and flirting and going to parties and 'getting with' people, it's so hard to escape this idea that you just have to be dating or seeing someone to be a functioning member of society, rather than just sat in the bath looking at whoever's-house-you're-at's medicine cupboard. However, it's the heterosexualization of dating that actually makes dating as a queer non-binary person so difficult.

★

It's a warm summer's day and I'm taking a break from looking iconic, and I'm stood outside my local coffee shop smoking my life away, on my phone, when an attractive, short, brown-haired, brown-eyed man comes up to me.

'You look amazing, you're really like a work of art!' he tells me. I nod in agreement.

'Thanks!' I exclaim sharpishly, not really making a lot of eye contact with him, but noticing that he's wearing boat shoes. An interesting choice.

'I don't normally do this but...,' he begins. My eyes look up into his face as he's stood in the sunlight. Leather jacket in June? Another interesting choice, but I'll look past that.

He continues.

'...I'd love to take you out for a drink sometime if you fancy it? I know this is super random but I've just moved to a nearby town and I'd love to get to know you.' It's like a fairytale. My *Sex and the City* senses are tingling, and in the most Miranda way, I nonchalantly agree. He takes my number, shakes my hand (weird) and we move on. We walk away and then do that awfully embarrassing look back, where we both do it at the same time and then essentially give ourselves whiplash by spinning our heads back around to make it look like we weren't silently checking each other out. We do this about three times, knowing that it's as much weird as it is hot. Smugly I return to my seat and continue with my day, feeling even more beautiful than I normally do.

The text comes just half an hour later. He thanks me for speaking to him and offers to take me out for a drink the following day. Now I love spontaneity, and anything that resembles a scene from a '90s rom-com, so this to me was ticking a lot of boxes. Also, he was pretty stunning, so I was on board with the hilarity of a random wine date with a random man who seemed to have liked what he'd seen, and vice versa.

The bar I was meeting him at is literally opposite my flat, so as a precautionary measure to make sure I didn't look like a glamorous floater, I stood in my window and waited for his message to say that he was there. It got to 5 p.m. and he messaged me to say he was just approaching the bar, and as soon as I'd pressed send on my relaxed yet anxious reply, I saw him walking into the bar, still in that leather jacket, even though it was still June. He was upstairs out on the roof terrace (brownie points for good seat choice) and had ordered himself a pint. I approached and realized it was heinously busy with people from university, but I looked past that and walked over.

And this is where it began. 'It' being him essentially being a gross man. What's new. First of all, if someone invites me out for a wine, and they get there before me, there are two options. Wait for me to arrive, and then we can order drinks together, or swim further down the river of spontaneity and order me a, what I call, 'surprise wine'. He'd done neither of my preferred options and was already sipping on a gloriously vibrant pint of something that probably comes with masculinity already injected into it. A testosterone froth, if you will.

As I sat down and began conversation, I noticed that his air of charm and mystery had slipped slightly, and he was positively rigid and stern in his approach, as if I'd just asked him to come and meet me to talk about his mortgage, or worse yet, football. I looked past it at first, telling myself that it was obviously because I am just so beautiful that he couldn't even begin to pluck a sentence out of the air. But as I chose my wine, we were sat in an incredibly toxic silence that felt like everyone around us was listening to. Trust me, I tried to squeeze some everyday conversation out of him as I chose my drink, but yet I was left un-quenched and with a lot of pith. I left, ordered my wine and said to the barwoman that I was on a hilarious random date with a man who had 'picked me up' in town yesterday. I briefly explained he was being a bit odd and silent, and she reassured me that if anything went awry, I could come down and get her. Brill.

When I returned I realized he'd moved my chair. Where I was before sat at ninety degrees to him, now it was more of an acute angle, and a seemingly forward touch. I sat down and realized that if I didn't cross my legs over, I would be banging knees with him, which I reserve only for date three. I crossed my legs and proceeded to sip on my wine. He then decided to take the table number marker in his hands and began to twirl it in his fingers. It was a brashly painted wooden spoon with the number twenty-five on it. Bearing in mind, a lot of this has all been done in silence, and I'm mildly stressed and unsure a) why I'm here and b) what he's doing with the spoon. Do men stir their pints with big wooden spoons on dates now? Who knows at this point. He then proceeded to very visibly take the spoon under the table, and begin tapping my thigh with it. And in that instant I knew precisely what this was. He was a chaser.

Now, a chaser is someone who actively looks for trans or non-binary people to essentially just sleep with, because they've fetishized us and our aesthetics into something that they want. It's all for them. It's something that some trans and non-binary people don't mind; however, a lot of people, and me included here, find it one of the hardest things about dating and relationships.

I looked at him over my glasses and giggled. I regretted it instantly. It's an example of how it's so easy for femme-pre-senting people to shrink themselves in situations where they either feel vulnerable or are in the presence of someone that they want to impress. It's also a sign of a lot of other things, like uncomfortability; however, in this instance it was a giggle that said, 'I don't really know what to do now because I've realized you just want to sleep with me, and I've only just bought my wine.'

'So when are we going back to yours then?' he says.

My eyes are in the back of my head rolling more times than a washing machine on the final spin cycle. But I remain poised and calm, because turning down men is often not as straightforward as it might appear to be.

'We've literally only just got here, tell me about yourself, do you normally pick people up outside coffee shops in the middle of the day?' I expertly said. Calm, yet a distraction from the way that his mind was evidently going.

I know what you're thinking. Get the hell out of there. Why are you still there? If I were actually embodying Miranda from *Sex and the City*, I would've thrown my drink over him, made him buy me another one and then thrown that over him. But pretty much all situations in life are not fictional, and they come with real-life consequences, and real-life dangers. Especially as a non-binary person who presents visibly femme and visibly queer, I needed to remain alert.

He then continued by telling me about his life, and I'm not going to lie to you, it was incredibly boring. I almost wished I'd never asked because he then turned into one of *those* guys who just talks about himself for forty-eight minutes and then when he finishes talking doesn't even offer a gratuitous 'and you?' Awful. As the conversation dried up again, he started talking about my tights. He said they were gorgeous. Red flag. It was a sign that he was here for one thing, and one thing only. The pressure to voice my opinion on the sexual comments was growing. At this point I'd just been laughing or ignoring him, or telling him to stop it but in a fairly non-aggressive way. Nonetheless, I had asked him to stop.

He abruptly told me to hurry up so that we could 'go back to mine'. I'd foolishly told him at the beginning of the date that I only lived across the road, hence why I was so quick to get to him initially. A harmless statement now manipulated by a man into making me feel bad for not sleeping with him because 'I only live over the road'. Red flag number two. Red flags three and four came when we then decided to leave, and I said that I was just going to run to the loo first. I ran downstairs to the bar, and told them that he was being bizarre and overtly sexual, and I wasn't too sure how to say no.

In your head, logically, it's so easy. You just say no. Calmly and normally you just decline the offer, as if you have been asked if you want to drink a cup of cold piss or eat some Turkish delight. You just say no. But in that moment it can become so hard to say no. Something takes over your mind and it constricts your thoughts into thinking that saying no is the worst thing you could possible do. That you're being too dramatic, or rude.

Just like everyone else, there can be lots of different reasons why we are dating. We might be looking for a genuine relationship and something serious, or we can be looking for something non-committal and fun. There is nothing wrong with any of that at all. But the intent of other people who ask to take us out on dates often comes from a place that's purely sexual.

We left the bar and I walked him to the train station as an offer of goodwill, which was foolish. Essentially I was doing a 'sorry we didn't shag' walk. How entitled are men that their actions make me feel like it's necessary to apologize to them for not wanting to have sex by walking them to their end point? He turned, telling me that I'm not his type. That I'm not feminine enough. That (and this is my favourite because it happens far too often for my liking) he didn't want to have sex, he just wanted to 'chill at my flat'. This over-defensive attitude did nothing to hurt me and did more of showing me how un-intelligent and misogynistic this man was. I said my goodbyes, and I was feeling upset. Not because I liked him. Not because I thought he was 'the one'. But because that ship had clearly sailed as soon as I strutted into the bar. That the excitement and prospect that I'd had hours before was now a distant memory, one designed to remind me of my ignorance and foolishness.

I was upset because there's always that part of me that just wants to go on a 'normal' date. And that word is really important. The word normal, in the world of relationships, has come to be synonymous with cis, white and heterosexual. The social upbringing that we've had – where we have not been exposed to the beauty of queer relationships and have only been shown the many ways in which you can be in a heterosexual relationship – has meant that non-binary people are often not seen as worthy enough to be taken on dates, or not seen to be a group of people who are looking for love, or affection, or care. It's either sex or nothing. We are told to be a box to tick off of many people's 'sexual bucket list'.

The skewed viewpoint of trans women being 'shemales', often initially seen through porn, and only being subservient to cisgender straight men, means that a lot of men see trans women and femme-identifying people as a group that are 'up for grabs'. We are seen as being the bottom of the food chain. A group that would 'take what they can get'. And often this can result in us taking on this role just so that we can have that immediate affection and closeness with someone. That instant gratification of approval and feeling wanted. Even though we know the motives behind it are transmisogynistic, it often doesn't matter, and we fall into traps of allowing ourselves to offer our time, energy and sometimes our bodies to men who wholeheartedly don't deserve us.

I have learnt to know that my time, my energy, my body, my presence and my aesthetic are precious. We should all take this mentality when it comes to dating because it doesn't only save us time but ensures that the people we do then decide to spend time with are worth our time, our energy and our space. It can be hard to acclimatize to this mindset at first due to the years of social conditioning that have told us we have to 'give people a chance' and 'take risks'. But when taking risks can lead to potentially vulnerable situations, why should we have to endure this pointless exercise when we can move onwards and upwards to people who will make our lives better, rather than more complicated?

It's about making these dates and these spontaneous wines devoid of any ambiguity. Ambiguity is something that a lot of people would describe as 'the mystery' of the date. The 'who knows what might happen?' This idea has become so romanticized that it has eroded the boundaries that are so pivotal in ensuring we are safe and comfortable when dating. What we need to start doing is asking, whenever we are going into a scenario where we don't know precisely what it is in terms of 'is it a date or is it just a friendly wine?', so that the ambiguity is out of the window. It hasn't even come into the room.

This has really helped me to ensure that I see dating not as something that is in the hands of someone else, and to take back control of the dating world and the dating scene, and reacquaint myself with my power to know that I am allowed to be in the driver's seat. To be able to flirt and be confident and intelligent and articulate on my own terms. However long it takes for each of us, we all need to remember how powerful and unique we are, and that we don't need to rely on other people to feel fulfilled. We don't need to wait for someone to come along and sweep us off our feet. We are too busy carving our career paths to the highest level they can possibly be. We are too busy surrounding ourselves with the best and most enriching people possible. We are too busy being bloody iconic to worry about conforming to the heterosexual ideals of conventional, normative relationships. Build yourselves up to a point where the only way you should allow someone else to join you or forge a relationship with you is if they're on your level and are adding something to your life. As non-binary people, we are unique and beautiful. We have fought through a lot to get to where we are, and a lot of us are still making our way through the world, one step at a time.

Someone asked me recently, 'Do you think everyone should be a little bit queer? If our message of gender non-conformity and the fall of heteronormativity is actually seeping into the cisgender/heterosexual world, shouldn't we embrace people who once identified as straight, but are now opening themselves up to the queer world?'

I was taken aback by this. Is the queer agenda actually trying to destroy heteronormativity, or are we just trying to allow heteronormativity to relax a little and loosen its binary restraints? This was brought about after one of 2019's *Love Island* contestants came out and discussed that he wouldn't 'rule out' dating men, after rumours circulated on the show that he was in fact gay. It made me think about the ways in which queerness is often pictured and positioned as something that is so far away from heteronormativity. I think the first thing to acknowledge within situations like this is that in the instance of the *Love Island* lad, he is a very traditionally hyper-masculine man who is now within the public eye, so his answer had the essence of scripture about it. It was pre-crafted and aligned to fit with his new image, and so often outing yourself as gay, or queer, is deemed to be an 'image killer' or 'career ender'.

Dismantling the rigid structures that we all live by, cis/trans or queer/non-queer is important, and if cis/straight people feel like they are now questioning their position or feelings on their sexuality or gender identity, then that's absolutely valid and okay. What isn't okay is when people insinuate that they may be open to same-sex relationships but want to try and avoid any relation to the LGBTQ+ community because they feel like that could tarnish their image. I've always thought that everyone is a little queer, and it's the rigid shaming that we have had rained down upon us from day one that stops many of us from actually exploring how we feel. So if you're cis and straight and one day you feel like you are attracted to someone you've not been attracted to before, or if you one day feel like you want to explore your gender identity in ways you've never thought about before, then BRILLIANT! But remember and acknowledge your position, and know that you have a community just an outstretched palm away to help you. Rid yourself of that shame by embracing the community with open arms, at whatever pace you feel like you want to. It doesn't have to be a grand, revolutionary moment but allow yourself to explore that part of yourself that you're figuring out. You owe yourself that.

★

As a twenty-two-year-old who lives in a metropolis of people and art and culture, it seems bizarre to me that in every other part of my life, I try and take in as much as possible, and share as much with the world around me. But monogamy tells me to conform to one person for the rest of my life? If I'm honest, even before I truly expressed and lived with queerness on my sleeve, the whole idea of finding one person always seemed alien to me. The notion that there is one person out there that is destined to be with you until your last day seems a little too fairytale to me. But, on the flip side, is polyamory for everyone?

One thing that is of paramount importance when it comes to being in a polyamorous relationship is that communication is key. If you're in a relationship that isn't fully open, in a communicative sense, then how is it going to be open in every other way? There also needs to be a real foundation of trust there. That essentially is true for all relationships, but one where you're able to form relationships and connections with other people needs to have that strength and truth behind it even more so.

One of the only long-term relationships that I've been in was with a polyamorous person, and it brought up a lot of questions in my own head. For me, the overwhelming feeling was that although I knew monogamy was flawed and might not work for me, going head-first into a relationship with someone who already had another partner was potentially a dive straight into the deep end. However, I was determined to be fully on board SS *Poly*.

My three-month relationship in 2018, which still holds the record as my longest, and first, had a ridiculous whirl-wind of a start. I woke up that morning to a rogue message from Matt. A person who I'd not spoken to before. So like every self-respecting person would do, I checked to see if they were hot. They were. Brilliant.

We spent the whole day talking, and they informed me that they were in London for the rest of that day only and were heading back to their home out of London in a few hours. As they day progressed I was aware that we were talking non-stop. It got to around 2 p.m. and they informed me that their train home was at 3:30 p.m. I was about forty minutes away from their location. Now, I'm not sure if it was because of the copious amounts of caffeine that I had ingested, or the fact that after an intensive FBI-style search of their social media I came to the conclusion that their cheekbones could in fact cut parmesan cheese into thin strips, I decided to be spontaneous. I messaged them letting them know I was on my way to meet them before they got their train.

God, I'm just so wild!

I'm going down the escalator to enter the train station they're at and I'm in full panic mode. What am I doing? Who am I? Why do I make all living situations that I am in so dramatic and over the top? Am I okay? Is my heart supposed to be beating this fast? Why am I asking myself all these questions out loud so all the passers-by are probably wondering what the fuck is that person doing shouting at themself?

I saw them, instantly stopped in my tracks and gasped, and proceeded to hide behind a pillar. Classic. I stood there and took my headphones out. Checked myself in the reflection of my phone and adjusted my outfit, popping the collar on my infamous 'Nancy Boy' leather jacket just to really affirm that I am in fact, that bitch. I walk over. Every inch of my brain and my body is telling me to run away. To walk straight past. Pretend that I'm not me. But with this face, that's fairly difficult. I walk over and we see each other. We stare at each other and smile. We hug, and it was a different kind of hug. It was a hug that said, 'I know you'. It was a hug that said, 'we've hugged before,' even though we've never met. It was weird, but in a good way. It was actually very weird, and I didn't really know what to do in that moment. It was like I was meeting someone that

I'd known for years and was finally reconnecting with, but also literally only meeting them for the first time. Getting to know them in that instant hug. Their smell to this day still makes me scream internally if I smell it on someone else. The hug finished and we started talking, and I'm sure you're all aware of this weird phenomenon that I like to call *'when you've been talking online all day and then meet in person and don't really know how to continue it even though you have a million things to say'*-syndrome.

Our hands weren't just lingering by our sides. They were touching each other but in a way that was like our hands and our limbs were also meeting and seeking the other person out. We were talking about their journey. Their time in London. My face. I couldn't help but tell them how ridiculously piercing their eyes were. I have a thing for eyes. Not necessarily a sexual thing, but just like a 'thing'. I looked around to notice the spot we were in, because I knew this was going to be a moment, and no matter how this whole debacle ended, I wanted to remember where I was stood when this happened because I'm a parody and have to ensure every moment of my life is at least like a rom-com that only made it to DVD release.

Now here's a quick hilarious thing about kissing, and any future flames take note. I love a good snog, but when you've got the whole entirety of approximately thirty-two people's makeup on your face, despite being stealthily secured on with enough powder to mattify the SUN, it's still fragile and easily moveable.

We kissed. I was mesmerized. I've kissed people before but not in a way that might have meant something. As someone who is often fetishized, when I first started engaging in dates and meeting people, a lot of it was sex based, and the kisses felt like nothing. They felt like something that was just a precursor to the main event. Often like kissing an orange, or the back of your own hand. Something that you might have at the beginning but you don't overly have a passion for it. Like olives.

This felt different. It felt impassioned. The way that we had met was so unconventional and spontaneous that the kiss was the icing on the cake, as well as the cherry. I truly had never felt this connected to someone before and our hands went to each other's torsos. We were having a proper moment in front of people rushing to get the Tube, and I didn't care. I didn't care who saw us. I forgot momentarily about the vulnerability of our queer bodies showing affection in public. I forgot about everything. I even forgot about the fact that my makeup was ruined and was definitely going to be all over their face. I felt wanted. I felt needed in that moment, and that's something that I'd not felt before. To this day I still thank Matt for that.

The kiss stopped and I surveyed the damage. Their face literally looked like one of my old makeup wipes, and I tried to wipe the lipstick off their face. We were still holding hands, and we just stood in shock. What was happening? Why was this all so dramatic? Whatever it was, I knew I wanted it to continue. They went for their train and I ran to the closest Boots and asked them to try and rectify my face, which turned into me just asking the lovely woman at the Chanel counter for makeup remover. I left, went and sat on the floor outside the station and cried.

Holding hands for me is something that is so important. I think it's because so many people take it for granted. Cisgender, heterosexual couples holding hands is essentially a privilege, but they take it for granted because they've never been told they can't. I'd gone to the Cambridgeshire countryside where Matt lived to stay with them four days later. When they took my hand, I screamed internally. That battle inside, of very, very, deep, dark, internalized queer-phobia that is telling me not to do this, but also to hold on to them for eternity because it's the best thing that's ever happened. What is it about hands that is so sexy? The fact that they can go anywhere is probably a bonus.

We walked towards the ruins of a castle or something;
I wasn't really properly listening but just pretending that
I was because I couldn't really concentrate on anything
palpable. I was adamant that this wasn't my life. Someone had replaced my beautiful body with someone else's
equally-as-stunning visage, and they were now in my place.
This couldn't be happening. Me? A trans individual feeling
mildly happy with someone who is also trans and just being
romantic and cute? Are we sure?

Fuck. We're getting married. I can feel it. This is literally
it. All hyperbole aside, I'd never felt so comfortable with
someone in the space of literally four days, ever. I'd always
heard that when queer people fell in love it was all at once
or not at all. It was intoxicating. It was all consuming. I later
found out that the stereotype of queer relationships being
'all consuming' and rapidly intoxicating often occurs because
of a lack of boundaries and a yearning to be wanted, which
can blind us into only seeing what we want to see. However,
I couldn't help but feel it all at once. We got up, walked
through the ruins and towards a bird sanctuary, where there
was a choir in the nearby church singing. I literally couldn't
make this up. I was walking through a park, in full bloom,
with a choir singing metres away. The sun was out. Their jaw
was literally deadly, and they had a leather jacket on. Our

hands hadn't parted since they conjoined, and I was having a moment. There was an intensity that I enjoyed, but later realized was toxic.

There was a moment when, only around two weeks after we'd met, we were at mine in bed. I was lying there wondering how in the world I had ended up here. They were cuddling me, and I was just staring at the ceiling. They had told me they loved me earlier in the day. I knew from countless episodes of pretty much any sitcom that if I didn't say it back instantly, it would be a 'thing'. Even though I didn't feel it, the thought of losing them, and not having this security of another person, was not something I wanted to witness for myself, so I said it back instantly. We settled into going to sleep about half an hour later. I turned the lights out and in the darkness, felt like I was going to explode. My eyes were open to the darkness in front of me and it felt like it was sucking the life out of me. As if I wasn't me anymore. I couldn't sleep, or continue knowing that I didn't love them, and that I'd just lied to them because I was worried that I would never have this ever again. I leant over, switched the light on.

'I'm sorry but I don't love you,' I said as our eyes fumbled back into the light.

Three months later, it was over.

I was overcome with emotion. I remember the next day sitting on the train thinking, 'Am I really going to end this relationship after twenty-one years of never having anything?' Thinking about what I'd waited so long for and then to have it but also be the person to end it was so bewildering. 'I'm never going to feel romance again, and I'm going to end this and that's going to be it,' I thought as the train ground to a halt.

I think often when relationships end, there's a very binary sense of who was right and who was wrong. Who made this end, and who is the bereft party. But with Matt, it felt different. The intensity was too much for me. I felt trapped. I let Matt and their emotions, their feelings, their troubles and everything about their life become a part of mine, meaning I felt every single part of their life. It was worryingly boundaryless.

But although it ended, it doesn't mean that I didn't learn a lot about myself, and in this scenario, a lot about polyamory. Matt recently shared with me that they define polyamory as something that allows them to *be able to express your love for the myriad of identities, bodies and minds without any confines or restraint. Who has the right to tell someone that they can't consensually love more than one person?* Just because it ends, it doesn't mean you can't learn something from it.

If like me you feel as if you're not ever going to find happiness, one of the best things we can do is to deconstruct that notion of happiness and really look at where it comes from. Acknowledge that we are putting our lived experiences up against a pretty boring and rigid structure of hetero-normativity and cis/euro-centric ideals of what constitutes a relationship. Although she has troubling politics, and bad taste in winners, Ru Paul is right when she says, 'If you can't love yourself, how in the hell you gonna love somebody else?' Allow yourself to learn about the parts of yourself that are beautiful and transcendent, because only you have those. Learn about the strength and the love that we have within the trans community, and how intricate and bespoke it is. De-centre romantic love and take it off the pedestal that it lives on. For so many of us, wanting and desiring a relationship comes from a deep-rooted desire to appear 'normal'. But we can only be our version of normal, no matter how clichéd and Disney that sounds. We have a desire to be wanted. Obviously not all relationships adhere to this; however, often when we are frustrated that we are single or not in a relationship, we feel like having a relationship will complete us, which just isn't true. Yes, it can allow us to have great happiness and a good shag, but it should never be something that fills your glass only halfway. It should be a situation that essentially allows your glass to overflow. Try it. Delete your dating apps, get your hands off of Grindr, and for a week take time to not think about it, and see how you feel. A lot of the time we feel worse about our romantic situation because we are constantly searching for it through apps and methods that aren't built for trans bodies, reminded of the lack of accessibility that comes with being trans.

Now, the friends that I have are a very close-knit group of individuals; however, they all provide me with the love, nourishment, care (sometimes a shag) and allyship that I used to crave all from one person. No one person can provide you with everything.

9 THINGS I WOULD SAY TO A NON-BINARY PERSON WHO WANTS TO START DATING

1. Don't try to find someone who you think is going to fix you. This isn't a Coldplay song.

2. Remember that not everyone you go on a first date with is going to be your future life partner. Although it's easy to feel like you can have an everlasting connection with someone in those first few hours, know that it could just be because you have a mutual identity that you're relating to, or worse, you're bonding over shared trauma,

which can sometimes be an example of where boundaries are needed.

3. Don't order noodles. Just don't.

4. Don't change yourself in order to make someone else more comfortable. This predominantly focuses on your aesthetic. It's so easy to feel like you shouldn't wear something or present yourself in a way that you think could alienate your date, but honestly, ignore that. It's internalized transphobia, and if they don't like it or want you to change how you look so they feel more comfortable, then they're making your job easy to know that they're not the one for you.

5. Remember that you're the best. Call it ego-centric, but if this person is going to be in your life, they need to be adding to your greatness. Adding to your excellence, rather than making you concentrate and shrink yourself into a smaller, less authentic version of yourself.

6. Remember that you don't have to talk about your identity all night. It's easy to feel like that's something to talk about because you both might have that shared lived experience, but know that you're more than your identity, especially your trauma.

7. Bloody have fun.

8. Learn to take romantic love off the pedestal that we are told it exists on. Love from other people in your life is also as strong and often a necessity to be able to navigate the world as a non-binary person.

9. Don't fetishize other people. Just because we often face prejudice when it comes to dating doesn't mean that we can't also have societal bias and dating 'preferences' that are actually harmful, such as 'only being attracted to black people' or 'no fats, no femmes'. Unlearn and educate yourself on these issues before dating, because otherwise you're a part of the problem.

Similarly to the way in which non-binary can be seen as a self-definitive term, the ways in which we observe romantic relationships are something we should begin to class as self-definitive. Love and romance can feel like an entity that is so intrinsically linked to heterosexuality that it homogenizes all people, no matter what gender, into a strict set of rules and regulations. If you want to have thirty-eight partners and sleep with all of them, babes you rock and roll. If you don't want any partners at all and just want to live free with your self-love and a packet of custard creams, rock and goddamn roll. If you want just that one person and still adore the notion of the fairytale, you go and get that glass slipper back. I've recently been reading and speaking to older trans people about how when they were in their twenties, they were much like myself and others. They never thought they'd want that conventional life, or that life that seems to assimilate their identities. However, when they grew older, they realized that they can still be as forthright in their politics and settle down and get as much pleasure from the Made.com sale as they do from a quick shag.

The Stapler and the Jelly

Mental Health Awareness Day is always a time where we are all able to reflect and give insight into the ways in which we are living with our own mental health. It is also a chance for some of us to openly share our problems, sometimes for the first time. Mental health has become a flourishing topic of discussion, especially in the circles that I exist within. As a twenty-two-year-old, it's often hard to look back and think of the times when these conversations weren't happening, as the existence of people of my generation has been essentially parallel to the social media and digital revolution that we are currently in. For me and many other people, this parallel means we can feel like – despite the fact that these conversations about mental health are necessary and helpful – we are constantly exposed to these difficult and raw discussions. The rawness and reality of this constant sharing of the mental health of people we have in our orbits means it can often feel like a mirror is being held up to us, asking us a plethora of questions not only about how we can support others, but also about what state our own mental health is in. Sometimes, we just don't want to answer those questions ourselves.

For trans people, the statistics are hard to swallow. When we read about our own community in a very numerical and academic way, it can feel like we are having an out-of-body experience. As if we are not in fact part of that community and are looking down upon this group as numbers instead of people. Percentages instead of lived experience. Don't get me wrong, this information is invaluable, and new, and allows institutions that offer mental health services and our NHS an insight into the people they are often forgetting about or failing. But this knowledge doesn't mean that the information is not sometimes hard to digest. Twenty-four per cent of respondents to the National LGBT Survey that was carried out in 2017, and released a year later, had accessed mental health services prior to them taking the survey. The statistics for the rest of the population state that 1 in 6 people, or around 16 per cent, of the general population have a mental health disorder; however, the difference in the statistics for LGBTQ+ people is that 24 per cent have accessed services. Nearly a quarter of LGBTQ+ people have actually taken a step further and asked for help, which is arguably one of the biggest steps there is when it comes to our mental health. What we can then assume is that there are still hundreds of thousands of LGBTQ+ people who haven't asked for help, therefore indicating that mental ill health among LGBTQ+ people is far more prevalent than what the statistics are showing. Not everyone is going to want to share their data with people. Some people lie, especially if they're not out, or don't feel protected. It's also dependent on privilege, as often institutions carrying out these types of surveys have unconscious bias. Meaning the results can favour those with more privilege, such as white/cis/able-bodied/non-religious queer folk.

In a similar way to LGBTQ+ hate crime statistics, there is a huge number of instances where we as trans and non-binary people don't report issues, or we don't ask for help. If we look at hate crimes, one of the main reasons why many queer people don't report the crimes that happen to them is because of an awareness that nothing will ever come from it, or that the police won't understand what they're telling them, or – often for people of colour – there is a lack of trust and faith in the police system due to their failings for marginalized groups in the past and the institutional racism that is still perpetuated through unlawful killings and abusive, unsubstantiated arrests.

The similarities here with mental health services are something I have definitely experienced when it comes to the fear that these institutions are just not made for us. They're not crafted and created to allow non-binary people to feel safe and able to share their innermost thoughts. This isn't necessarily something that they're doing on purpose, but rather it is something that they're turning a blind eye to due to the binary way in which the medical systems in the NHS and in private clinics operate. The trickling of information that we learn as our own beings into the spaces that we work in, the spaces that we socialize in and also within our family units is something that will inevitably create the change that we want to see in the world. The wall that people face, however, is that they recognize that they're just one person within a whole cognitive system that is making decisions far above where they are situated within that system. But what we need to say to those people who decide that they're too small or insignificant within an institution to make change is that that is essentially how non-binary people feel all of the time. That we are just one small group of people within a huge binary system who are trying to flip the script on the way that the rest of the world sees and interacts with gender. Right now, the non-binary community needs these undercover allies within the biggest organizations, such as the NHS, so that when we do come to access services, we don't feel like there are countless barriers preventing us from even getting in the door.

One thing I always think of when it comes to my own mental health is the image of when someone has suspended a stapler inside a mound of jelly. Yes, that's right. A stapler in jelly is the one visual depiction of my mental health that I have chosen to put into writing here for you. If you don't know what I mean, pop the book down now and go and have a quick Google. It's a whole entity, suspended in a translucent fruity casing that you can see through. To the untrained eye, it may look impenetrable. The stapler is being held by the matter around it; however, one slice through and it will fall and no longer be encased by the fruity support that it has found itself within. Similarly my brain and my mental health is something that is a whole, living, breathing thing, and instead of being surrounded by strawberry jelly, it's being held together by me. In this analogy, the stapler is my mental health and the jelly is me, my thoughts, my brain and my actions. It's being held by something that you can see. You might have to squint to work out what it is, but you can see it. It's tangible. You know exactly what it is. But just like a stapler in a mound of jelly, sometimes you can't see mental health for what it actually is. You have to spin it around, squint, hold it up to the light and study it to truly realize just what you're looking at.

Our mental health can often feel like this. When we are living such busy, stressful and nuanced lives, we can feel like the thoughts and feelings that we are having are actually just normal. They're simply part of our existence. A side car to our main body, in which the negative feelings and coping mechanisms we enact on a daily basis to deal with the way the world treats our bodies become normalized in our own heads. Commonplace. Everyday. I think many non-binary people believe that our lived experience and the impact that has on our mental health is something we can't change due to the fact that the staring, the comments, the misgendering, the abusive language and physical attacks aren't anomalies. They're everyday occurrences, so we often stop trying to navigate the after-effects in our minds when these instances happened because we are so used to them. We become numb to our own trauma. Being numb doesn't mean you don't care, it just means that it doesn't surprise you. It doesn't shatter your world or throw you off centre. It just sits on top of you. You don't really feel it, but you know it's there. Like when a part of your body becomes numb, you can see the pressure being applied, but you can't feel a single second of it. This, for me, is why it became so hard to realize that my mental health was so bad, because it had become so commonplace in my day-to-day life to feel down that I didn't actually realize that my permanent mood was now, in fact, being down.

One of the biggest things that impacts my mental health is the way in which I am treated in public spaces. I think that's why it was so difficult to deal with my poor mental state, because changing the ways in which we are treated as a non-binary person in public spaces is not always within our control. We sadly can't curate the landscape that we are surrounded by all the time, and therefore face the wrath of the oncoming world at such a pace that we aren't even able to truly acknowledge the strength at which the prejudice is coming. It's like being on the beach, surrounded by a million grains of sand, and even though you have worn the right thing and you feel like you're prepared, or that you're okay, the sand will still find a way to go down the back of your neck and hit you in the spots you didn't realize it could get to.

People often say to me, 'Yeah, but the people looking at you could just be looking in adoration or appreciation. You don't always know the people staring at you are doing so because they're against you.' And my response is always the same. No one should feel like the second that they step outside of their house they're here for anyone else's enjoyment, entertainment or pleasure. Unless that's your aim of the day, or the pleasure doesn't bother you, then personally for me, I don't really care what the motivation is. This notion that we should be able to accept people looking at us doesn't sit right. When you are stared at, gawked at or spoken about, at every living moment that you're outside in public presence, no matter what the intent, it gets to a point where you can't just accept that this is the way that we are supposed to be living.

I remember the first time I heard staring at people called violence, by the amazing Alok Vaid-Menon, and the penny dropped there and then for me. This is violence that is impacting me and my mental health every day, but this idea that we are just supposed to turn a blind eye to it meant that I didn't fully understand the impact it was having on me. I was gaslit into thinking that this was not a problem that was actually happening and that I was being paranoid. That people weren't staring. That that's just what it's like when you live in a major city. I'd told myself time and time again that this wasn't something I was experiencing, because I was more than that. But learning that that was wrong, and acknowledging what was happening and is happening every day, was a really important step for me to be able to see the impact it was having on my mental health. I could now see through the jelly, right at the stapler, and see what it was. Trapped.

Relationships of the romantic kind are commonly intrinsically difficult to manage in a mental health capacity. I've never related to the idea of same-sex couples, and despite seeing same-sex couples within the media or over-simplified rom-coms kiss under the stars, it's never felt like that was something I could see myself within. Not because I don't have self-worth, but because the trope of same-sex couples, specifically within TV and film, is often two white, cis, conventionally attractive people who fall in love. I never saw femme-presenting people who were assigned male at birth (AMAB) fall in love with people and have that journey, so as a teenager, and still in part now, I felt like I was rendered unlovable. Or at least not able to exist in love in a way that everyone else was allowed to do.

My previous, and only real relationship, with Matt, off of Liverpool Street Station, was something that had ticked a lot of boxes, and for me it was the first relationship that had a sincere effect on my mental health. The ways in which we met and the first date were all so romantic and idealized that it felt like my whole life had been waiting for that moment, and my brain and mind were overflowing with emotion and jubilation. I was so swept up in the rom-com nature of it that that's all I could think about. I think that for many non-binary and trans people, when we experience love or any feeling or life event that fits a heteronormative mould, we are conflicted. On one hand, we feel like we are adhering to assimilation politics and can be frustrated at the fact that something so against what we practise and align with is making us feel so content and happy. But on the other hand, we feel like we are actually doing said act radically, and although we were running through the rain and kissing a stranger in the middle of a packed central London train station, it was two non-binary people doing it, and we were doing it in our way. But the twist in the tale for my mental health during that relationship was that I became infatuated with the fact that I was able to have a relationship, just like everyone else. My happiness came from the fact that I was able to 'just be' like everyone else. Truthfully, and looking back now, ashamedly, I was happy to assimilate because it made me feel more 'normal'. Growing up and being socialized and raised in a transphobic society as a trans person doesn't mean that you bypass that transphobia. It becomes an internalized poison, dripping and feeding into all the actions that we take until we begin to start the process of unlearning. So often when we experience conventional successes we can feel like we have finally got to a point where we fit in. We are accepted. We've DONE it. (This is all bullshit.)

This is why my mental health was affected so detrimentally during my time in the relationship, because only looking back now can I clearly see that not only did I enjoy the fact that I was being adored, loved and appreciated, but I fed off that notion of feeling like everyone else. It was like I had finally got an invitation to the cool kids' party. For so long, I'd seen everyone else around me getting invited and having fun, whilst I'd been sat at home playing *Cooking Mama*. But then, I'd felt like I'd been handed the VIP ticket, into my own personal booth, and I was able to experience what everyone else had been feasting off of for years. It turned into not just rose-tinted goggles, but a full rose eye transplant. I was literally so infatuated with Matt, and more so with the feeling of 'being in a relationship', that I would brush off and dismiss any red flags that arose or issues that surrounded the relationship because any attempt to take me out of this new VIP arena would be squashed without a second thought. And that's where the problems with my mental health began. I'd acquired too many red flags within the first three weeks that I was now constantly having arguments with myself about the future of the relationship, and the main reason that I stayed with them for so long was because I was terrified that I would never have this again.

I remember dramatically sitting on a windowsill of my new house that I'd just moved into. It was 2 a.m., and my sister had given me a bottle of Prosecco two months before as a graduation present. I had deemed that snogging a random person at the train station, me then going to their house for date number two and now having planned for them to come stay with me for date number three was enough of a reason to chain smoke out my window and drink my way through a bottle of Prosecco. I had the house to myself, so I decided to speak aloud a pros and cons list. This was pretty much how I spent the whole time of our romance inside my own head. Debating whether it was a good thing or a bad thing. Acknowledging the red flags but then quickly stubbing my cigarette out on them because 'they loved me!' and 'the sex was great'.

Pros:
- They actually like me.
- They have a great face.

- They're also non-binary.
- The dick is good.
- The dick is actually great, let's be honest.
- I've always wanted to hold hands with someone in public and we do that!
- They have a hamster.
- I can't stop thinking about them.
- It's nice to feel wanted and loved.

Cons:

- They're at the beginning of their journey of identifying as non-binary so it's fairly emotionally intense on that front.
- They live outside of London.
- They're an addict.
- They look better in (some) of my clothes than I do.
- It's taken over my brain.
- I can't stop thinking about them.
- They want to have sex more than once a night.
- They want to have sex straight away.
- Sex??? (Can't believe I'm thinking this is a con but it is.)
- Being new to a polyamorous relationship set-up is a lot to navigate, especially in a first relationship.

The part of my brain that knew these red flags were actually concrete reasons to stop this from continuing was still computing with me. However, the intoxicated and romantically saturated part of my brain was stronger. I decided that, yes, the cons were bad, but this was new and I was 'overthinking'. Bollocks. If you ever think you're overthinking, you're not. I plunged the rest of the bottle, part into my mouth and the rest into the fridge with a spoon in because I'd seen my mum do that once.

I continued, and my mental health ignited. I was on fire, but also couldn't realize that I was on fire. I just thought this was what it must feel like to be 'in love'. I couldn't concentrate on work, my friends were being routinely ignored, I was centring everything that I was doing around this person and I was naive to the consequences this would have. It wasn't healthy.

This was a common theme for me throughout my late teens and early twenties when it came to online dating. I put too much pressure and hope on being able to get into a relationship, so I could feel wanted and 'normal', that when it fell through or didn't go the way I planned, my mental health would nose dive into a family-sized trifle. I was using other people's love and romantic persuasion as something that could fix me of my 'wrongs'. To make me feel more societally palatable. To quench my thirst for normality. When in actual fact, I now know that that's one of the most unhealthy tactics we can employ when it comes to dating. It's a fairly universal viewpoint for a lot of people: that when we are feeling low or vulnerable, we seek solace and that boost from other people. But as non-binary people, often we have that lingering internalized shame, which takes that feeling of inadequacy and multiplies it by a thousand. This then leads to irresponsible ways of dealing with the shame, or the fallout. Mine were sex and alcohol. Constantly hooking up, going to saunas, drinking red wine when I knew I didn't need to. Ignoring people, lying to them about where I am and what I'm doing. Who I'm doing. Craving that feeling of desire and want from someone in a way that I knew didn't come with expectation or longevity, just instantaneous abandon. Wanting to feel desired, or hot, or sexy, just for a moment. But I didn't tell a soul. I just continued to find that fix of pleasure, that instant enjoyment. But all this did was lead to more trauma. More feelings of being out of control, meaning I was left vulnerable to hands that knew how to control me. How to control my body, but this time for their enjoyment. For their entertainment. To not be listened to, whether that be yes or no. Or no. No. For me to be something they could tick off a list that only they were writing, adding to the end of a sentence rather than putting a full stop.

What I learnt from that experience, though, is that dating and being in relationships is never something we should use as a tool to make ourselves feel complete. If we are feeling incomplete or low or that we need to address an issue that is to do with our mental health, we should do so off our own merit and as our own people. It doesn't mean we can't ask for help; it does mean that the intention and motivation for such improvement shouldn't come because someone else has told us to or because we think it's going to make us more attractive to other people.

It's okay to not want to deal with your mental health. A lot of the conversations that we see happening on a mass media scale around emotional issues such as depression and anxiety can often make us feel like talking about our problems is the only solution. That sitting down with someone, whether that's a friend or your diary, is going to completely solve all your problems. Don't get me wrong, it can be a massive help, and a great start to addressing and analysing our problems; however, for minorities, and especially those such as non-binary people and people of colour, and those of us who are institutionally undermined and persecuted, it can feel like you're just talking into the wind. That our words are just that. Words. That they hold no power or resistance to the structures that be. Yes, we've been able to share and talk about the institutional transphobia that has meant we feel down, but we know that when we wake up tomorrow morning and hear the wind, these institutions aren't going to have fallen or completely erased their colonial and persecutory history that they're still pedalling into the present. This is why things like Mental Health Awareness Week can feel like they actually don't do anything for us: because it's often a group of cis, white, able-bodied, straight people talking about their mental health problems and how they battle them. It's not always accessible. Actually, it very rarely is.

During university, I went to my first ever counselling session about my mental health and the ways in which it was impacting my workload. (This was also as a result of a dubious online semi-romance that I'd had that had also led me to spiral.) It was helpful because it was with my university, so I didn't have to pay, and the waiting times were minimal compared with the NHS. To my glee, when I filled in the forms to attend, there was a trans option and also an other option. Like most forms, I scribbled underneath something about being non-binary and hoped that it would land in the lap of someone well equipped.

My first appointment was an assessment. An assessment of what I was there to talk about. Not an assessment of my gender identity. We spent the first hour-long session talking back and forth about how my very lovely therapist had never had a patient who was trans or non-binary and that she didn't necessarily know everything about gender and sexuality. This meant that the first session was spent with me answering all her questions about being non-binary. What it meant, when I first started to identify as such, how long I'd been identifying and all of the other ninety-eight clichéd questions that arise when you out yourself as non-binary. Although this was frustrating, and definitely something that I didn't need to do, I felt it was necessary for her to understand me more. And maybe it was necessary, because we then went on to have six incredibly fruitful, dynamic and powerful sessions that truly helped me through a particularly dark time. But this brought up the issue of accessibility again. Most people don't have access to free mental health resources, and trans people have to join the queue of millions of people within the bowels of the NHS mental health waiting lists, waiting to be seen. Even when we are seen, we are still often met with not only indifference or a lack of education, but also prejudice. Countless times, non-binary people have to spend their first sessions explaining their identity, to be met with hostility and questioning of their very existence. Told to change, or told to go private. Even if you do manage to find someone within the NHS who is open and educated, it's still not a tailored experience. It's still set up and built to allow cis, straight, white people the best chance of being able to have their problems sorted. It's not built for trans women of colour, or disabled non-binary people, or fat non-binary people, who just want someone to talk to. So the mass-marketed depictions of 'just talk about it' and 'speak to your local GP' often don't work for our most marginalized, and this shows the inability of and failures within our Government's mental health framework to ensure that all people are given the same opportunities and resources within our NHS.

★

Like many buzzwords of our time, self-care has gone from being a state of mind to a business. According to the *Harvard Business Review*, the self-care industry is estimated to be worth $11 billion. The industry has become heavily influenced by tech giants in Silicon Valley, with new self-care apps sprouting up every single day, and our beauty industry is now shifting to create all kinds of potions that are supposed to allow us to drift off into a deep state of 'self'. But how are we supposed to navigate this? Surely since it's become its own industry, it's now failing working-class people, as the correlation with commercialization and spending money to achieve bliss makes it appear that if you can't afford a new lavender room spray, you're not allowed to self-care? Or if you can't afford to just 'take a break' and go on a mini-holiday over a long weekend to Soho Farmhouse then you're just not going to be able to deal with your mental health, and that's 'not our problem'.

It's essentially telling the working classes that it is *your* problem, and we can't help you with that. But it's also failing our most ostracized in society, some of whom are most in need self-care and self-attention. In a similar way to the way in which our mental health services are advertised to us, self-care has become homogenized by the rich, white, straight, cis, able-bodied elite into more than just a state of mind. It's become a strict rule book, and if you aren't following, then it's your own problem if your mental health is then in turmoil. That if you aren't able to just 'dream, believe, achieve' and drink turmeric lattes in the morning and wake up at 4:30 a.m. because that's the 'optimum time to achieve the most progressive day', then I'm sorry but we can't help you!

As non-binary people, often these methods of self-care just aren't accessible. For example, one of these tools for self-care is going to the spa, so I decided that it seemed like a piece of advice that I could take. I booked myself into a nearby spa with the last remnants of my bank account, ready to be transported into a new dimension of self-adoration and tranquillity. But in actual fact, I'd forgotten in my self-care haze that spas are actually one of the most gendered facilities known to humankind. Treatments are split into men's and women's, presuming quite naively that a man wouldn't enjoy a relaxing facial or exfoliating all-over body scrub. Or even that people who aren't cis white women would dare walk through their doors. It quickly turned from a time to locate and realign my somewhat messy chakras into an episode of endurance. How long could I sit here with this woman's hands on my face without screaming about the incredibly gendered way she was towards me and my skin after presuming that I was male? As she gave me statistics about men's skincare and the thickness of male skin, I decided to just not reply and pretend that this was all fine and that my skin would be smoother than a car bonnet.

In actual fact, all that I ended up with was a loss of money and mild stress, and my skin still resembled the smoothness of the Brexit withdrawal process. I know this is a fairly jovial example, but in reality, the self-care arena isn't accessible to all, which results in a lot of us going two very different ways. We either set up and found our own online resources that share practical advice on how to be marginalized and navigate self-care, which has truly shown the brilliance and importance of social media sites such as Instagram. Or we end up not even bothering, and use age-old and fairly toxic coping mechanisms that are more at our disposal, such as sex, alcohol, drugs or another quick trick that can allow us to keep pedalling through.

Self-care isn't an eye cream or a new duvet. Yes, refocusing your efforts on fairly ritualistic actions like buying new skincare, or ensuring you eat more fruit and veg, or buying a cock ring, can work in making us feel better, but for me self-care is a concept that never actually has a solution. It's not something that we can just do, and then the world feels better and brighter. It's something that we have to continually practise, and hone, so that we can begin to find things enjoyable again. And if that's buying new skincare or experimenting with owning house plants, which every single gay I've ever come across now does and acts as if it's their first experience of being a parent, then bloody do it. If it's reigniting a love for an old hobby you used to have as a child, then do it, and enjoy it. But know that it doesn't have to tie into the capitalist narrative that says that if we have more things we will feel better. Because all that does is fulfil you for a day or two, and then when you realize that the £29.75

you spent on a new calming aromatherapy kit isn't actually making you feel better, it drops you back into the spiral of guilt. This time with less money.

6 THINGS I WOULD SAY TO A NON-BINARY PERSON TO DO WITH THEIR MENTAL HEALTH

1. It's good to note here that although sharing your emotional moments with fellow non-binary people can be cathartic, it's also emotionally intense, so make sure that if you are doing so, you've checked with the people you're speaking with to make sure it's okay to offload, because it can often be triggering to hear other people's stories when you yourself are not necessarily in the right place.

2. It's okay to feel angry, and frustrated. When we are experiencing so many unique feelings and emotions that our own institutions don't know how to deal with, it's only natural for us to feel angry at that. But don't allow that anger to sit. You can feel it, and you will feel it, but don't allow it to sit atop your mental space permanently. Channel it into something beneficial for yourself.

3. Take five breaths. It helps. (Thank you Samantha Baines and Gina Martin for sharing this with me.)

4. Don't ever apologize for saying no. It's one of the most powerful tools in your arsenal, especially when you're speaking with cis people.

5. Be present for other people within your community when it comes to their mental health. This is a collective time for us to work out how to deal with our respective mental health issues, at whatever pace is necessary. Share trigger warnings, and be wise to other people's states, but know that our shared experiences can be a true ease to each other's problems.

6. Know that it will pass. It will feel like it never will, but it will pass. I promise.

I'm not going to sit here and give you advice on how to find your own self-care, because I'm not you. All I can do is share what makes me feel better, and what we have seen time and time again that doesn't make people feel better, so that you can hopefully use this conversation as a catalyst to find your own *thing*. Mental health problems kill people, and that's why I find it so disheartening and disgusting that companies think the answer to this deadly disease is to get people to buy things. It's not going to work. Self-care and our own mental health are two entities that we have to sculpt and work out for ourselves, because our identities and inter-sectionalities are so bespoke. That, combined with the fact that our NHS and local community services often are failing trans people and not even recognizing non-binary people, means that groups such as cliniQ and Mermaids, who are offering truly life-saving and vital resources to non-binary people through counselling, therapy, sexual health services and familial advice, are fundamental to our existence.

My mental health over the past year has been the worst it's ever been, and like so many other trans people, I've not known what to do about it. I've tried conventional tactics and I've tried the commercial ones, and nothing has worked, and the guilt we feel when we are in that space is monumental. The shame of not being able to be fixed by what is fixing everyone else is just another example of how ostracized we can feel. But in actual fact, no one is being solely fixed by that, and realizing that for me was a minute moment of solace. To know that it's all just a bit of a lie doesn't necessarily fix your mental health, but it allows you to put into perspective your own situation, just for a second. I still don't know what to do with mental health, and I don't know how to feel all of the feelings that come with being an out, femme non-binary person. There are days when I don't want to be here. There are times when I wished I wasn't non-binary, but there are also times I am so thankful that I am. There are days when I wished I wasn't who I was, and there are times, so many times, when I just want to exist without all of the additions. Without the pressure. Without the staring, the name calling, the objectification, the accusations, the sexual assault, the intimidation, the belittling. But our gender identity and the beauty it holds and the power it ripples is never the problem. Say it with me. We are never the problem. Being non-binary is never the problem.

Life as a non-binary person can feel like you're constantly being pulled down the ladder when it comes to the impact on your mental health, because the societal prejudice, lack of accessibility and violence that we face based on our gender identity is cyclical. It's something that we don't have control over. That's why it can feel so difficult to seek help or believe in the help that is out there, because we know that even if we do speak about our problems with a therapist or with a friend, the second we leave that room and head out into the world we will still be greeted with the same problems. That combined with the oppression from other intersectionalities such as race, class, ability or religion proves again that there is not one way for us to be tackling this as a society. The solution comes from an embodiment of empathy. Empathy allows us to see other people and feel and resonate with them. And within the non-binary and trans community, empathy is drilled into us. It's why when we are physically together as a community we are so strong and united: because we have empathy for each other's lived experiences. It's why we sadly hold each other's hands that little bit tighter when we are about to say goodbye. It's why we make sure that we text one another the second we get home late at night. It's why when we greet each other, we hug for just that little second too long, and that extra bit too tight, because we know. We know what it's like. We know that navigating the world as a non-binary person is like walking through the world with a target not just on our backs but all over our bodies. It's why we are so understanding and able to listen to each other's stories, and feel them, and need them, and emote with them. It's where I've been able to find the most strength and solidarity when it comes to my mental health. It's where I've seen the light at the end of the tunnel and realized that we all have mental health problems. All of us. It's not something that can be fixed forever, but we have to ensure that our mental health is a priority for our survival. It's where I've been able to relax.

Don't forget to relax. Don't forget to breathe out. You're

allowed to breathe. You're allowed to exist. You're allowed to thrive. We are all here, as living, breathing, sickening proof of that, and although we might be struggling, we are here with you every single step of the way.

Underdog

There's not really any way to finish university without feeling like you're literally the only person in the world who doesn't have a job and you're falling off a cliff. It's a whirlwind of uncertainty, yet an abundance of freedom. The knowledge that you are now out of mainstream education and flying into the world of 'buy buy buy sell sell sell' is something that many of us feel, but we don't really talk about it when it's happening. We just pack up our squalid uni flats and sit there with the 39p and countless empty biscuit packets that we found under our old bed, wondering if we should go back to our home town or fuck it and just try and exist where we are living now.

After university I was in a situation that was far from what I had expected. After creating FRUITCAKE – a magazine I created in my final year of university – I was in a space that in my head felt like I had just won an Oscar. And to be truthful, it was probably the Oscar of the graduate world. I walked away with the dazzling statuette from the 2018 Graduate Fashion Week (GFW) Awards as a 'Future Talent in Communications' as decided by the GFW team and the lovely people at ASOS. A moment babes. It was for FRUITCAKE. The summer before I started my final year I had interned at Stonewall, where I met the incredible Sarah Moore. Sarah and I spent six weeks and Pride 2017 together, and I truly had never felt such love, warmth and strength in a work environment before. It allowed me to not only be myself, but for it to not be an issue at work, something I had always worried about. Leading into my final year, I knew that I wanted to do something queer focused for my final project. I was asked to create any business I wanted, and I decided a magazine was a good shout. I had always loved magazines and trashy tabloids, so I embarked on FRUIT-CAKE. A queer print publication celebrating the creativity, excellence and power that queer people hold, immortalized in print, twice a year.

I remember sitting in the crowd before the awards began,

in and amongst hundreds of graduates from across the country, all of us tucked neatly into the Truman Brewery, not really understanding how I'd got there, but also fully not expecting to win. And that's not just my Meryl Streep actor facade coming into full force; I genuinely didn't expect anything from it. As queer people, we often see ourselves as the underdogs pretty much all of the time. Any time that we achieve success or do something that is worthy of praise, we presume that we aren't going to win. Or if we do win, it's a fluke and they clearly got the name wrong in the hilarious oversized envelope. There's no in-between.

The awards are in full motion and it's been a good hour and my nerves and ass are throbbing. Suddenly the time is here. When I get nervous, I go one of two ways. Either I'm an absolute silent mess and kind of sit in pure stillness and quiet and don't say a word, or I start bopping my knee and commenting on things that are going on around me that are completely irrelevant. For example, in this instance I started twiddling my thumbs and shaking each knee against the other and kept muttering under my breath that this was 'all just a sick joke' and 'why did they decide to have a white stage and runway? What if people's shoes are dirty?' Future Talent in Communications, sponsored by fashion giant ASOS. The adorable Liverpudlian man from ASOS arrived on stage, with headphones around his neck, which I thought was really chic yet also felt like he'd just stopped by on a run and had taken them out briefly to adorn someone a winner. My brain wasn't able to concentrate for the first part of the explanation of the award because I was wondering why he still had his headphones around his neck. Was it like when Britney performs and she has her inner ears so that she can hear herself talk? Who knows. And to be quite truthful, why was I caring?

You know in award ceremonies on TV when they have that award that's like the lifetime achievement one, and instead of just reading out the name, they really slowly describe snippets of that person so that they reveal piece by piece who they're talking about? Well, this award wasn't on the scale of Barbara Windsor winning her lifetime achievement award at the Soap Awards, but there was that rather repulsively frustrating build-up to the winner. At this point, I kept turning to the person next to me, who was someone from my university who was also up for the award, and kept muttering in her direction that 'this was a joke' and 'what the fuck is happening? Why am I here?' Really keeping it professional.

'This publication champions difference, and looks at the ways in which the LGBTQ+ community—'

I fell off my seat. Even though at this point I definitely knew he was talking about FRUITCAKE, I was still very adamant that another queer person had been nominated and that it was going to them.

'The award goes to, for the brand FRUITCAKE Magazine... Jamie Windust.'

At this precise moment the people in the front row had turned around to look at me, and I realized that the camera man – who I hadn't noticed had been pointed to the side of me – was in fact talking to me. I exclaimed a very loud 'FUCKING HELL', and proceeded to then walk onto the white runway. I went up, tried to do a double kiss on each cheek of the man from ASOS and ended up just nuzzling my head into his shoulder, and proceeded to take my award. My main thought was 'don't fall over because Henry Holland is in the crowd, and although he has no idea who you are, it's probably best not to fall over in front of him'.

As I teetered off the stage in my stilettos and flouncy pink dress, we went backstage and I will always remember this conversation with the adorable man from ASOS because it's truly something I take with me through all the work that I do now.

Adorable man from ASOS: 'Well done! We really thought your magazine was something that hit the nail on the head right now of what people need. It's speaking to a community that needs that sense of community in print, and it was so beautiful to see. We all agreed unanimously when we saw it that it was the winner.'

Me: (Not really knowing what to say because his arm was around my waist so I was a bit preoccupied with not falling in love with him.) 'I just don't believe it. And not in a clichéd way. Like, I don't understand *why* I've won?'

Adorable ASOS man: 'Why don't you believe you could've won?'

Me: 'Because queer people are always the underdog. We never win. If we do win, it's never because we are the right person to win, it's because it's the "right time" to win, or because it's "on trend". It's something that queer people the world over feel because we are never celebrated, and if we are, it's rarely from organizations that aren't predominantly queer. Like, this is a pretty straight room so to win here just feels unbelievable.'

I don't truthfully fully remember what he said to me after I said this awfully self-deprecating statement, but it was along the lines of 'shut the fuck up, you deserve it', which was enough for me in that moment. It's true though. We never feel like we are deserving, and if we ever do succeed, it's in situations and spaces that are predominantly queer.

Infiltrating the straight cis world is enough of a win, let alone to triumph over the other people. For me it came from a space of being constantly undermined and disbelieved as a non-binary person in all other aspects of my life. To have your existence and identity constantly questioned is something that filters through into so many other facets of your life that it can feel like a drop of ink falling into a glass of water. Suddenly all of the other parts of your world that once seemed like they were crystal clear and straightfor-ward are now plagued by self-doubt and second-guessing. Throughout so many years of my life when I was in school, and growing up, I was never told I was good at something that I actually enjoyed. There was academic success in school; however, learning about trigonometry and how to make a white sauce were never truly passions of mine. To be told that you're good at something that you love doing is special, and I truly treasured that moment.

Being trans in the workplace is something that we don't discuss enough. Being visibly queer and trans in a space where you are still under so many rules that were most likely made by cis white men is something that results in the atrociously high levels of prejudice that we see in the workplace for trans people. One in eight trans people in the UK have been physically attacked by customers or colleagues

in their workplace within the last year and 50 per cent of
non-binary people specifically have hidden their identity
in their workplace because of fear of discrimination.[1] It's
the cold, hard truth that we have imprinted in our minds
when applying for jobs, and it can be such a deterrent for
so many people to even apply for work in the first place,
leading to frustration, mental health issues and financial
problems that can plummet us into depths that we never
knew possible. This is an instance where I do find myself
being envious of white cis straight men, and that's a real
rarity. Knowing that your gender isn't going to prevent you
from getting a job is a real privilege, and often why so many
of us who are non-binary don't even bother applying. It's a
privilege that is so often blind.

This, piled on top of the universal 'graduate terror' that
we feel when we leave university, was a cocktail that I was
not ready to stomach. It was so hard to explain this to people
without being gaslit entirely. As non-binary people, often
our lived experience with everyday situations is turned into a
space where we are told we are being paranoid, or overthinking the whole situation. But we know that that's not true, as
the statistics above exemplify; our lived experience of this

---

1   See www.stonewall.org.uk/system/files/lgbt_in_britain_-_trans_
report_final.pdf

situation is something that proves it isn't just a falsehood we are worried about. It's one of the biggest mental barriers that many face when looking for work after university.

One of the first times I was submerged (and nearly drowned) in the world of 'traditional work' was during university. During my degree we had that illusive period where we had to work within the fashion industry, and mine was for the grand total of eleven weeks, which I felt was extortionate. Did we really need to work for that long, unpaid, to just get a degree? I wasn't really in a position to say no, so I obliged and looked for somewhere to work. I didn't really know where I wanted to go, but as my studies encapsulated fashion business, and the many avenues that that can take, I decided I'd take a punt on fashion PR. As a huge lover of *Ab Fab* and also high-powered fashionable businesswomen, I thought it would be a breeze. Of *course* it would be just like it is in the films, only this time I was Anne Hathaway, and instead of *Runway*, I was working at a mid-tier PR firm in Shoreditch, where coffee cost nearly as much as my train ticket there. Just as Anne would've wanted.

There were many things I was concerned about that I had been assured would be fine because 'you're in Shoreditch!' and 'it's *fashion* darling', but I was still nervous as to what the 9–5 office life would be like. Would I be treated the same?

If I were to be treated like a sack of dirty socks, would it be because of my identity or instead because I was just another fashion intern amongst London's thousands who are literally crawling through fashion cupboards running on no sleep and poppers? Or both? Only time would tell as I crafted what I would describe as the outfit of a generation. My take, if you will, on a 'suit'. Ugly dad tie, tiger print shirt, yellow roll neck underneath and a yellow high-waisted denim jean, topped with what could only be described as a patchwork coat made up of different pairs of trousers. Brilliant.

To say that travelling from Surrey to East London every day felt like trekking from Edinburgh to Paris was an understatement. I was waking up at 4:30 a.m. to get into full Jamie glam, throw on the outfit that I'd planned the night before, walk to the station and then board the forty-five-minute train to central London, where I would then take another thirty-minute Overground train to Shoreditch High Street. Fortunately the PR firm was opposite the station, so as I emerged from the Overground station, at this point not even walking but just being so squashed by other commuters that I was being elevated from train to pavement by two pairs of shoulders, on my first day, I trotted up to the door quickly. I was greeted by a group of people that literally couldn't have been more disinterested to see me if they'd tried. Was it the dad tie? Were they not a fan? Did they not think the yellow jumper and trouser combo worked? Alas. Still fairly introverted and shy, I was not at a point where I was incredibly proud of my identity and didn't have that sense of empowerment that I have with it now. Due to my terror and lack of genuine social skills, I ended up just standing there for a solid five minutes before someone then decided to say hello and ask who I was.

My role at the firm was to essentially 'capture coverage' (truly if I hear the word coverage one more time in my existence on this earth I will explode). This involved going through social media accounts, articles, features and photo shoots that the products from the brands that we represented were in, screenshotting them, finding out how many people potentially could've seen that, and then putting it in a spreadsheet. This might sound interesting (if you're boring), but it was actually one of the worst things I've ever had to do for longer than ten minutes. Also, how the hell am I supposed to know how many people took the *Time Out* magazine that they give out on the Tube on one particular day, and then how many people might have looked at a pair of women's cycling shorts and gone 'oooh Christ they look good let's buy them'? Outrageous.

I realize that a lot of the treatment actually wasn't

because of my identity but was in fact because I was an intern. I was done. Only two weeks in and I was well and truly done. After spending those two weeks of buying my lunch and eating it in the bathroom (because I'm really that cliché), I came to think about the ways in which my identity was being treated here. Was it safe? Was I being misgendered? Call it a self-appraisal. Overall it was a safe environment. There weren't any raging, obviously bigoted people within the team, and one of them was also queer, so I felt like I had at least one ally. However, micro-aggressions were in full force.

My favourite comments were from the young woman who ran the social media. She was a fashion blogger and stylist in her spare time, and very into fashions that I would also wear. Pretty much every day she would comment on my outfits. Not necessarily in a negative way, but definitely in a scrutinous and analytical way. My favourite phrase (I got to a point where I was actually counting how many times she would say it consecutively) was the 'GOD, you look better in that than a WOMAN!' A thinly veiled compliment. Not something I could necessarily fly off the handle at with how frustrating it was, but also not nice enough for me to thank her profusely over. It inherently implies that I am a man, but also that I shouldn't be wearing it. That by me wearing it, either I am trying to be a woman, or only women should be wearing it, and that my wearing it *and* looking incredible is an out-of-this-world achievement.

After three weeks I decided enough was enough, and I was going to try to find somewhere else to work. One day I saw an advert on Instagram for a volunteer role that was available at Stonewall UK. As I sat on the loo eating the burrito I got every day from the van outside, I knew this was it. This was what I wanted. To be quite honest, what I needed. I applied by email and awaited a response. Four days later, I was invited for an interview. My brain exploded. Here we go; all aboard my ticket out of here to a new queer haven that would allow me to just be, and also pass my degree.

I will never forget the feeling of being inside the Stone-wall offices for the first time. I'd never properly been in a space that was unapologetically queer. As someone who didn't partake in the nightlife scene, there was rarely time for me to actively be amongst fellow queer people like this. I felt euphoric. I literally felt like I didn't have to explain a thing about myself. For many of us in life, and in work, we are met by cis people who feel like they're entitled to know literally everything that they don't understand, there and then. If they don't understand something visually, they're going to ask, or they're going to be standoffish with you until you explain it to them. But inside the walls of Stonewall, with their beanbags and areas that are just wall-to-wall cushions, I felt safe. The interview went well, and I was told that I would hear back within the week. A few days later, Stonewall offered me the position on a part-time basis, which actually still aligned with my degree certification and also meant that I didn't have to work full time. Truly a win-win. My time at Stonewall was invaluable and truly allowed me to experience a work environment that was devoid of stress or anxiety based off of how I identify. But it did taint my view of the world of work. I had essentially started my journey into the world of work in queer utopia. What I defined as the crème de la crème. So although it was stupendous, I was now worried that I'd set the bar too high for future career opportunities. Would anywhere else fulfil me or sustain me with the safety and validity that being inside Stonewall's walls gave me?

This introduction to working within queer spaces was the main motivation for me ensuring that whatever I did in the rest of my career, it was focused around queerness and more importantly, queer people. I wanted to surround myself with the community in all that I did because of the safety and comfort that it gave me.

Now, I'm in that position of having one of those awfully millennial 'portfolio careers'. I'm many things a lot of the time, and some things more at certain points in time. For example, as I'm writing a bloody book right now (hello from the past), I am more of a writer than I am a public speaker. However, during fashion week, I'm more of a model, so the ebbs and flows of the career that I am forming are something that I am constantly learning about, both within myself and also as a businessperson. During university, I never thought that I would be a freelancer. In the UK alone, there has been a 66 per cent rise in people aged 26–29 adopting a freelance career, and specifically within the creative industries it's something that is incredibly commonplace. Many people use their spare time to facilitate their side hustles, with that quickly becoming their main hustle. But it's not an overnight phenomenon. As someone who essentially fell into freelancing, and then decided to take it by the reins and really roll with it, it was one of the hardest and most terrifying things I've done. That leap of faith into a world where you don't necessarily know at the start whether or not it's actually going to formulate into a long-term career or just remain a side hustle is borderline excruciating.

9 THINGS I WOULD SHARE WITH SOME-ONE WHO WANTS TO BE FREELANCE

1. Get a therapist.

2. Create a great playlist of songs that aren't going to distract you and will keep you focused on the task at hand. Try Ludovico Einaudi.

3. Don't wait to work out how do to your taxes until you feel financially secure.

4. Although tempting, don't quit your job as soon as you have the idea to be freelance. Whilst working, build that network and spider's web of people that you could potentially work with until you feel it is strong enough to support you when you do take the leap.

5. Know your worth from day one. Don't sell yourself short just because it's your first job or your initial experience working with larger companies or brands.

6. Talk to your peers. Find other freelancers and you'll quickly realize that all we talk about when it comes to work is how much we got paid, who pays well and how long it takes them to pay.

7. Be aware of people who will just want you to do things because you're non-binary, and be aware of whether or not you should be taking up space there. Have conversations about how your workplace needs to be more diverse,

apart from gender, and ensure that if, for example, conversations about racial discrimination are happening, there are people of colour in the room. Give up your seat.

8. Know that the institutions and corporations you're working with, or for, are set up with a history of transphobia, misogyny and white supremacy cemented within them, so you're going to have to work harder than others, and that's frustrating. But know that your work is equally as valid as your counterparts, if not more. Don't be disheartened by setbacks based off of gender discrimination. Know your rights, call people out and if necessary, move on when you're able to and feel safe to do so.

9. Know your identity isn't always your USP. Don't feel like you have to constantly take your trauma to the bank. Do work that includes things that you know and lived experiences that you've had, but also channel your passions and loves into what you're doing, as that's equally, if not more, important.

That last one is really important and poignant for me. You could argue right now I'm contradicting myself by writing a book about my identity and my lived experiences; however, the difference here is that I chose to do that. I have autonomy over writing about my experiences and my stories in a way that feels comfortable and okay.

Over the past year, I have learnt so much about the work that I am doing, as well as its correlation to my identity and my community, and the impact that that can have as a whole. Not just on me as an individual, but the impact that the work that I do has on our community. Don't get me wrong, I'm not the messiah for non-binary people, but often as a white, skinny, able-bodied, non-religious member of our community, I am seen as a mouthpiece. Someone who speaks for all, when that is never possible. Feeling that I am often told I am speaking for the community has never come from a place rooted in ego, but has come from a place of privilege, as my experiences are seen as more palatable. A perception of queerness that is digestible. The past two years have been an awakening of my own privilege, and how I can use it to open the door wider for everybody to be heard.

We all make mistakes in our careers, and I certainly have made my fair share, but whatever industry you're in, realizing your mistakes and the reasons for them, and ensuring they don't happen again, is something we should all strive to do. Investigate the errors and don't allow them to be repeated. Much like my work with FRUITCAKE, I use my platform now to ensure that the door is thrown wide for those who have more to say. Ensuring the space for queer/ trans activism isn't dominated by white people, and thin people, and able-bodied people. I have the privilege to be able to have the conversations with media, with agencies, with brands, about what they need to be doing better when they speak about non-binary and trans people, to ensure they don't just paint a palatable picture.

Don't get me wrong, as a model, working with global brands as the face of their campaign is a dream come true. The number of times I've walked down the road to school envisaging it as a runway or a photoshoot that I am the star of is too many to comprehend. But specifically Pride season this year showed me that working with brands, or media, or any capitalist-facing, large, multinational corporation is not the 'peak' of activism. So many people within this world see 'brand activism' as the goal that we are all aspiring to. The star on top of the tree. A collective feeling that this is what we do it all for. But that's just not the case. It's bollocks. I want change. I want non-binary recognition legally, socially and institutionally, and being the face of a shoe brand's Pride campaign isn't going to do that. It's fun, don't get me wrong. I love it. Like I said, as a model, it's a side of my career that I enjoy doing, but like a lot of relationships this year, I've learnt to de-pedestal it as the best way to create social change. Using capitalism to electrify a message has benefits, such as large-scale visibility of the issue, representation across the globe, and young people seeing themselves rep-resented in institutions they've never been seen in before. But it's so often a conflict of interest and can have more negatives than positives. Like many trans professionals, I just want to be seen as a model, or a writer, or a speaker, rather than having my identity prefix what I'm doing. It's been a tough ride to decide whether or not to try and exclude my identity from the things that I'm writing or speaking about, but I now realize that decision is mine to make. We have the capabilities to speak, write and do whatever we want, and if we decide that speaking about our experiences and our community's experiences is something we want to do, then we should be allowed to do it. But always, always remember that we don't have to.

Especially for those with privilege within queer spaces, we need to make sure that we know when we are taking up space with our work and when it's important to pass the mic and amplify other voices. Allow yourself to just have a career. It doesn't always have to be queer-centric. Your skillset isn't intrinsically linked to your identity. You're a whole, intelligent, brilliant and skilled person outside of your gender identity. Know that you're allowed to thrive in whatever you want to do, and by being that person who is thriving, you allow other trans and non-binary people to see that it is something we are all capable of. We need to be holding the hands of our trans siblings, throwing them on our shoulders and ensuring that are all successful, powerful and happy in this outrageous working world.

This is definitely what Dolly Parton was singing about in '9 to 5', right?

Lukewarm Stains

I'm writing this after being physically assaulted in central London. It's raining but that didn't seem to stop
them. It was busy but that also wasn't a deterrent. I wasn't
wearing any makeup, but that didn't seem to halt them in
their tracks either. I was on the phone for an important job,
and debated whether or not telling them down the phone
what was happening, but like most times this happens, I
decided to continue walking and pretend that I had no
idea what was around me. Around my body. Around my
literal presence on the street. Not that it matters, but I'm
in flat shoes, a bomber jacket, a roll-neck jumper and smart
trousers, and a pink beanie. No makeup. For me, a look

that allows me to sink into the streams of people that pass through the streets every day. They follow me down one of the UK's busiest streets, throwing stones and calling me a 'gay boy'. I continue walking. I don't turn around. I continue to my destination. I stop at the traffic lights and hear two tall white men telling them to fuck off. That they're being outrageous. I'm in two minds as to stop and thank them or continue to get myself away from the situation. I decide on the latter and continue to cross the road, stopping briefly to turn around as I enter a coffee shop to check that they're okay. That it hasn't escalated. I catch the eye of one of the men who has stopped to reprehend this group of young men and smile. He doesn't return the smile and walks away. I order my coffee, and within minutes the event is out of my mind. The coffee runs down my chin and I wipe it away. Quickly gone. Forgotten about. Just a slight, lukewarm stain remains.

Roaming the streets without makeup on or appearing in the manner that I have done for so long is new, and for me is not just a time saver but a sad solace in some ways. It's a way for me to feel like I can assimilate, but in a way that allows me to breathe. It allows me to not have to second-guess my actions, or my route, or my words. Apparently not. I was foolish to think that just because I wasn't decked out in my usual blush contour and stars collaboration that I was safe. I was still visibly queer, and visibly femme, even if that outward expression didn't come from a four-inch mince down the street. It was still there, still with a target on my body to let people know that I am supposedly inferior. A moment of reflection to realize that any outward notion of non-conformity is still seen as an infringement on the lives of others, rather than a concept that allows those who embody it to adhere to their own version of conformity. A conformity to your own body, your own mind and your own set of rules. Conforming to your truest self. A notion that will free everybody. However we choose to present ourselves to the world as non-binary people, whether that be visibly binary or not, why are our own ways of living seen as bottles on a wall, ready to be shot down one by one? Smashed into a million tiny pieces and left for us to put back together, piece by piece, day by day, only to be obliterated again the next.

Anger has played a large part in my life. It's something that I feel more deeply and more passionately than any other emotion, yet like a lot of the things that we've discussed already, the numbness to my own anger has become commonplace. I feel the anger, and I hear it, yet I forget about it most of the time. Like a pirate with a parrot, it just kind of sits there, loud and colourful, chirping in my ear. Making me remember that it's there, but also becoming a permanent fixture of my person. I think anger is something that is truly terrifying but also necessary. A lot of the time we don't have control over when it flares and when it's just left to rumble along alongside us. Our worldly experiences allow it to flare, but we are often not in control of the ways in which we are seen or treated, meaning that the feeling of anger that we know is so strong is always at the start line, looking at an amber light. Ready to go. In lieu. Coming to a halt or ready to shoot upwards, it's always primed and ready to cease or explode, and for many non-binary people who outwardly present to the world in a way that may cause questioning or confusion from our cis counterparts, the reactions that we garner can mean that our relationship with anger is something we are constantly aware of.

I don't think people realize when they look at us, when they stare at us, when they laugh at us, when they whisper about us in tones that only we can hear, that instead of sadness we feel anger. It's such a hard feeling to try and explain. That feeling of knowing you're being spoken about. Looked at. Shouted at. Discussed. That's what it is. So often when I get onto the underground and sit down, a general discussion appears in the carriage about my person. As if I'm at a job interview, or I'm a loaf of bread on the shelf and I'm watching people decide whether they want me or not. It fucking hurts, because if we were to stop and challenge these people, we wouldn't make it down the street. We'd be stopping every ten seconds, asking why. Why did you do that? What was that for? Why do you *care*? It's an infestation of the brain, like tiny ants walking around inside of your head, every time picking up another friend along the way and creating swarms. Constantly walking, moving, reminding you of what's just happened, but not preparing you for it to happen again. Every waking second we are on edge. We are primed, ready for it to happen. We can't look down the road because catching people's eyes means having a front-row ticket to watching our own take-down. Watching people spit words full of venom, or naivety, or both, about you. I wish I could tell people to take my name out of their mouths. To take my body out of their mind. To just stop, before I do.

It's an anger–sadness hybrid, but anger is more tangible and fiery. It's easier to see and can sometimes feel easier to deal with because it's omnipresent. But what is a life if it's consumed by trying to deal with your own anger, caused by people who have no idea that they're creating such a furnace with their words?

I've just been on a massive scroll of my social media, to try to piece together the first time that I felt like I encountered prejudice. Truth be told, dear reader, I couldn't tell you when it was. There wasn't really a time when I first realized that this is prejudice; I just kind of felt it rise and then it found somewhere to rest. Behind my eyes, it kind of sat. I think back now at how there was prejudice during my years in sixth form, as there is today, yet I didn't see it as much as I do now. I didn't feel it as much, and that's surprising because at that age and in that environment of peers who were all sixteen and seventeen and figuring out their next steps, it was a hotbed of criticism and analytical voyeurism. But I think that's where being young and being stubborn and being bold and learning about what you feel brilliant doing, and what you don't, is so freeing. It's a time when, yes, there is hardship, and yes, there is fight, but it's also a time when we are able to explore ourselves in a way that it can feel harder to do when you get older. It can feel like the weight of the world has suddenly appeared at your door and is asking for a piggyback for the next seventy years. It can feel like you're suddenly unable to wear lipstick and heels or a suit and tie because you've got bills to pay or post-Brexit Britain to navigate.

But when it does get all too much nowadays, I always take myself back to that younger version of myself when I was trying on those heels for the first time. The first time

I went and bought a lipstick and brazenly put it down on the counter all on its own, with no fear and no care in the world. That's what I take myself back to. That clichéd notion of youthful naivety. When my biggest care was if this lipstick will smudge when I drink coffee, rather than if this lipstick will smudge when I'm punched in the face. When my biggest care was whether or not I'd be able to walk to sixth form in a four-inch heel and not get tired, rather than if I can use this four-inch heel as a weapon if I need to. Just for a second, I close my eyes and remind myself of that youthful energy and also plot it on the timeline of how far I have come. Of how, despite that glint of terror, I managed to overcome it by having the self-belief and self-adoration to be able to say to myself, 'fuck it'.

It's all well and good saying that prejudice is other people's problem, but when it's signed, sealed, delivered to your doorstep every day, it's hard to remember that this isn't something we have to dismantle. Again, in a similar manner to the ways in which we are told to self-care and deal with our mental health, this mainstream cis-washing of societal problems tells us to just 'move on' and 'know you're worth it'. All valid statements, but not necessarily compatible with the non-binary experience. The thing is, we know we are worth it. We know that we are valid; we don't have to be told these things as if we don't know our own power and strength. Like a lot of problems that we face within our binary segmented world, we have to work out how to deal with the problems we face on the spot and on the go. The irony of there not being a rule book on how to live outside of the rules.

★

My first job was working in a very small department store in my local area. Think of it as a shop that thinks it's Harrods but is actually a very mild-mannered and slightly prettier looking charity shop. It was one of those ones that is owned by the 'big family' in town, so was named after them and meant that all of the two-hundred-and-four generations of said family worked there in some capacity. Goulds. What a shit name. But I loved fashion, and needed money, so my first proper job was being a retail assistant in the menswear department. I was there at the weekends and got to wear a suit, so it was a great time to be alive in my book. (For some reason I loved looking incredibly smart at this period of my life. My school uniform was always immaculate, and the thought of undoing a top button and letting my tie loose seemed like the end of the world, so getting to wear a grown-up suit to work was truly orgasmic.)

The layout of the shop meant that menswear was a small section situated with a till in the middle, with a view of the beauty section and all the glorious makeup counters that sat like little dumplings in a stew opposite. White women would circulate them, spend hours debating over what eye cream to purchase, and then leave with a neatly bagged overpriced pot of lies and trot back to their Agas. That kind of place. I'd just started to wear light makeup at this point, and I had a plan of action from day one as to what I wanted to do here. I wanted to be one of the makeup-counter girls. It was like looking at a group of supermodels in kitten heels, glamorous and elegant, tidying their makeup displays and knowing all there is to know about BB cream. I wanted it. Fuck that, I needed it. I needed to be one of these glowing figures of retail gold.

I started working there over the summer in-between school and sixth form, and once I'd begun sixth form, my style and femininity were starting to form, so the suit felt odd now. I remember having to get ready on a Sunday morning and putting on my suit and tie and not feeling right. Feeling like I'd just put on some weird armour that didn't really fit anymore. I'd paint my nails and wear a little more concealer than necessary to counteract the masculinity that I was supposed to be performing and would trot my way to work. This moved up from nail varnish to a lip-coloured lipstick, then to a two-inch heeled boot, then to a bracelet, and more and more was adorned onto my body to align with how I was beginning to feel about my own identity. I took my time for my own safety and sanity, but I loved it. I didn't really care that much about it, and I loved how it made me feel. Sadly, and honestly unsurprisingly, the white cis rich family that owned the department store weren't best pleased. I was asked to take off the nail varnish and the lip-coloured lipstick and be more 'normal'. I adhered, but only slightly, sliding the bracelet up my forearm so I knew it was still there, but they didn't. A secret bracelet; how MI5 of me.

After six months, I decided I would take the plunge and ask to move over to the beauty counter. I wanted to be there. I needed to be there. I'd started to wear more concealer, and mascara, and spent most of my time stood on the very edge of the menswear department chatting to the counter girls across the non-existent barrier about what was new in and whether or not they thought I should wear more. They loved it. I loved it. We'd chat for what felt like hours, but was actually minutes, about makeup, beauty, skincare, what different products did, how much they were, what different serums did for your skin – the works. It was honestly like I'd just found the Bible and was reading it for the first time, but this time Jesus was talking about under-eye bags and hyaluronic acid. This was it; I needed to take my shot and ask to be moved over. There wasn't a vacancy; however, like all of the great movers and shakers of our time, if you want something, you have to show them a) that you want it and b) that it is worth them making a spot for you, even if there isn't one available. At the end of a Sunday shift, I accosted the manager in the staff room and told her I wanted to move over. Even if I wasn't behind a counter and was just on the till over in the promised land with the fragrances, that would do me just fine. To be stood on the marble flooring of the beauty hall rather than the wooden floor of the menswear department was a step I needed to take.

To say it went down like a lead balloon would be an understatement. The balloon here wasn't just made of lead, it had three titanium anchors tied to the bottom of it and was being thrown into the ocean from a much larger lead hot air balloon. She laughed in my face. Her reasoning here was that 'we aren't in London, Jamie, we can't just do those things here!' She spat at me, laughing in my face as she washed up her F-initialled mug in the staff room. F for Fran. Kind of like Flan, but she was less eggy. 'Maybe if we're short-staffed at Christmas, but I just don't think it's right, we're not in Selfridges,' she giggled, as if I'd just asked her if I could lie

naked in the window for this year's Christmas window deco-
ration. With my proverbial tail between my legs, I stumbled
off home, miffed and smelling like ninety-three different
perfumes that I'd tried on that day in my lunch break, the
only time I was allowed to venture over to the beauty side
of things.

A few months later, my makeup had gone from strength
to strength, and I was now rocking full foundation, brows,
mascara and a poignant red lip. My secret plan here was to
prove that I knew my shit about makeup and that it only
seemed right for me to be working in the beauty section
because well...LOOK AT ME. I'm beauty personified. I was
working a Saturday and it was busy, and I strolled onto the
shop floor to open the till, in all my femme glory. Everything
seemed fine. The male customers were shook, but that wasn't
anything new. Since I'd started working there, the men who
came to buy their white socks and baggy boxer shorts could
smell out any sense of femininity or queerness as soon as
they entered those automatic doors, and their disapprov-
ing looks and manner were now part of the job. I was just
about to go on lunch and was stood behind the till when the
manager came over to me and asked to have a word. Here
we go; this was it. I was being asked to move over to the
beauty hall. I strolled into the stock room, telling my brain

to remember this moment, because this was when my life was about to become the best it could ever be. I sat down on a box of Spanx and she sat opposite me, smirking, but also with pity in her eyes.

'What's all this then?' she probed, gesturing her index finger around my face to imply she was talking about my visage.

I laughed and replied with what now I look back on as hilariously arrogant, but a true statement all the same.

'Oh this? Just a little cover-up you know, thought I'd make an effort seeing as I'm dealing with men all day.'

Iconic.

'Well...,' she paused. The anticipation was growing. Was I about to get fired? Was I about to get promoted? Honestly James Wong couldn't have created this level of suspense.

'...you just look a bit much, Jamie. It's not just that you're wearing makeup, but it's not even applied well. You look... dead! And the lipstick is all over the place. Let's ask Debbie to take it off.'

I felt my lower lip tremble and she saw it shimmy as she was talking, but it didn't stop her from ripping me a new one. I started crying, and my mascara, which I'd stolen from the staff room, began to run down my face. She just sat there, unsure of what to do, kind of wanting to help but also just kind of watching and waiting for me to stop as if I were a set of Christmas lights that she was testing to see if they still worked. Squinting and waiting for something to happen.

'I'll go get Debbie,' she finally relieved herself with, and left me sat on the Spanx box crying. Big mood. Debbie quickly came in, gave me a hug and told Fran to go fuck herself, which was endearing. However, although Debbie had become my confidante at this time of makeup exploration, she didn't necessarily think Fran was out of line. She told me the makeup did look a bit shit, and that she could help me out. She took me onto the shop floor, onto her counter and sat me on the stool where customers come to get their makeup done before they go to the next PTA meeting. Fran came storming over.

'Get him OFF the shop floor, what are you doing?!' she shouted, again as if I were some stray dog they'd found in the stock room that was now parading around the shop floor for all to see. 'We can't have the customers seeing this. Get him in the back NOW.' It had got angry and I didn't really know what to do now. Debbie's counter had a little makeshift booth that looked like a mini igloo where she kept all the products, and she hurried me in. She took my makeup off – all of it – and then gave me some concealer to put where I wanted and to cover up where the mascara was still sticking to my eyes. I emerged back onto the shop floor, walked back over to menswear and continued my day. I didn't say a word. I didn't speak to Fran again that day, pretending none of it had happened. What got to me the most was the fact that I had so much self-belief and self-appreciation for the makeup that I had put on that day that being told you look like pure shit when you feel like you look like *the* shit is the worst feeling. Now that statement wouldn't even touch the sides, but then, at the beginning of it all, it hurt.

I continued to work there and did eventually make it to the makeup counter side a few months later. I think the manager felt bad for me, and also I still persisted, with that youthful stubbornness, and came back the next week with my makeup firmly back on. Being on the beauty hall was sadly a lot worse than I had thought. Although I was in my element with the products, giving advice and giving Sandras and Sharons tips on how to create that perfect smoky eye, I was also met with genuine overwhelming shock by some customers, who couldn't fathom that someone who wasn't a woman was a) giving them makeup tips and b) wearing makeup. I was laughed at. Security was called numerous times after people from school, who were a few years below me, found out that I worked there and kept coming to the front doors and just shouting 'poofter' through the automatic door. Every day, 'normal'-looking couples refused to be served by me because they didn't want to buy an eyeliner from a freaky faggot.

I eventually left the shop as I'd got another part-time job actually working behind a makeup counter in a neighbouring town, and I felt enthused and pompous at the fact that I was not only leaving but moving to the other family-run department store that smelled like dust, this time in a bigger and better job. One that they'd actually allowed me to have. Suck on that, Fran. I strutted out, and left a lipstick message on the mirror in the customer toilets like they do on *Drag Race* that just said 'Bye bitches'.

That was the first time I had experienced genuine harassment and prejudice from people who had no idea about me as a person. Prejudice that was based purely on the fact that I didn't look how they wanted me to, and was tied up in homophobia, transphobia and misogyny. A triple threat of public prejudice that I had never experienced before so viscerally. I'd experienced it at school, but bullying and name calling within those hallowed walls wasn't a new or rare occurrence. I'd grown accustomed to it. In hindsight, it all seems so awful, but at the time I was so resilient to it. I just didn't let it bother me. Sometimes I wish I was sixteen again and able to feel like that, hence why now whenever I do feel like the weight of people's words and eyes gets too much for me, I revert to my sixteen-year-old self, full of arrogance and *CK In2U Her* and don't pay it any mind. My inner cockiness comes out, and I just walk past, making a point of not hearing it. Even though I did. Even though it hurt. Even though I'll think about it when I'm taking my makeup off. Even though it'll sit at the back of my throat for a bit until another one arrives that allows me to swallow the previous one down.

Telling non-binary people to not care and brush off the micro-aggressions is like telling the Conservative Government to care for...well, anyone. It's not going to happen. It's also not realistic. Navigating the world as people who are constantly told that we are either wrong or don't exist gives people apparent permission to treat us like we aren't even human. So to tell us that we should brush that off is not going to work. If we could just brush off our oppression, I'm pretty sure we'd all be bloody sweeping left, right and centre. It goes back to the idea that people think we don't know our own strength and our own validity and power. We all know it. We don't need cis people to tell us we are valid, and we don't need to prove that we are valid. Although statements like this, granted, can often make us question ourselves, we still all have that deep inner awareness of our own validity and truth.

That never leaves you. Even though the words will erode you and chip away, we will always remember that we are never, ever, going to change to please strangers on the streets.

What does work is knowing that you and your identity, and your presence and existence right here, right now, in this literal second, is valuable. It's everything. You're living. You're breathing. You're existing, no matter what state you're in, whether you're feeling the best you've ever felt or the worst. You're here. There's another twenty-four hours around the corner that you're going to be a part of. You've just gotta get there. It's about sometimes really taking it back to basics and being like, okay, I'm alive right now, and I'm going to go home and have a cup of tea, and then go to bed, and then maybe a wank, and then sleep. To remind your brain that you're going to be alright. It's relentless out there, and often it can feel like you can't walk even two steps down the street without people pointing at you, or laughing at you, or telling you that you're a joke, or videoing you without your consent so they can appear funny on a Snapchat story, and I want you to know that none of that is your fault. The violence. That's what this is: violence. Towards our identities and our physical manifestations of our identities. And that violence is never our fault.

★

'I am sorry that the only way we have been taught to heal is to hurt.'

– Alok Vaid-Menon

'Well...what do you expect if you look like that? You've got stars all over your face and blush up to your temples. What are you actually thinking is going to happen when you leave the house?' is something that I am asked constantly. From trans people, cis people, any bloody person who wants to ask it will. When people ask me how I could stop the prejudice from happening, they flip it back around and slap me in the face with it, telling me that this is my fault. It took me a long time to realize that actually wasn't true. That being more me, and applying my stars every day, and sweeping the blush on my face, is only ever for my own enjoyment and fulfilment. If I were to do this every day for other people's attention or reaction, I simply wouldn't do it because of the violent nature of the reaction that it garners. It's that simple. My personal choice and experience with self-expression and creativity is so intrinsically linked to my gender identity that doing this every morning is an act of self-care and appreciation, and before I leave the house, it's truly euphoric and mes-merizing to me how beautiful, wonderful and non-binary I feel. My own collage of being non-binary. The beauty of self-definition.

Our creativity, our clothing, our makeup, our hair, our bodies are never the reason. It will feel like they are, and it will feel like if you didn't put that lipstick on, or if you didn't wear that jacket, or those shoes, or that hat, that you wouldn't be facing that prejudice right now. It's so easy to think that by taking all of that off, you will have an easier life, and sometimes that can feel so true. But we don't pres-ent ourselves to the world in the ways that we do, in the beauty that we have, for no reason. We do it because it *is* our truest selves. It's us. Our rawness, our realness, our identities in solid form. Without that, we are still the same people as before, but the bright spark of joy that comes with making yourself feel more you should never be put out by someone else's opinion of you. Remember that. Keep it in your pocket, in the back of your head, and hold on to it.

1 THING I WOULD SAY TO NON-BINARY PEOPLE ABOUT PREJUDICE

1. It's never our fault. Ever.

Spending time in community spaces with our fellow siblings, just being and existing without prejudice, has been some of the best times of my life. The non-binary and trans warmth that we feel when we are in those spaces is immense. Our community has a shared silence, which if it were to be played aloud would just say, 'I'm here'. I'm here for you. I'm here when you need me. I'm here alongside you. I'm here as an ally, and I am here now. Just entering physical spaces where trans and non-binary people are feels like coming home, and not in the England football kind of way. In a way that means so much more. We have created a space where we can momentarily escape the prejudice, and to do this means that we need to constantly be ensuring that we call out racism and xenophobia and Islamophobia in these spaces, so that our non-binary siblings of colour and faith can feel just as relaxed and at home in these spaces as we do.

That's something that is so vital to our collective energy in this world. We don't all have that magic switch to be able to turn off the violence, but the strength of allyship and empathy from within our own community is strong enough to silence the laughs and permeate the stares. It's enough to make us feel whole and complete in a way that no other act of community can. We're able to take our tongues down from the roofs our mouths, and unclench our jaws, allow our shoulders to sink down and to just breathe. You just did it, didn't you? Doesn't it feel good? We can't stop it, and that's the sad truth of it all. We can't go up to every single person who decides to shout at us in the street, or giggle at us behind their phones, and tell them that we are actually lovely people, and that we aren't going to be recipients of their abuse. But what we can do is to remember that it does not have to sit atop our shoulders every time it happens. Remind yourself, when it's happening, that very soon it won't be happening. It will be over soon. I promise. Our time on this planet, on this earth, will not be prefixed with the prejudice that we can't control.

Thempathy

Travelling with a suitcase is never fun. It's genuinely up there as one of my most hated activities, alongside watching darts and cottage pie. I was dragging my suitcase and limbs to the shoot for the second issue of FRUITCAKE and was over the moon. My friend Cat was meeting me there to help out, and I was on edge. I was releasing my first issue outside of university into the world, and it was a moment when I was able to really feel like I was cementing FRUITCAKE as its own publication.

What was more pertinent in my brain was the fact that this cover shoot was with two people that I held dear to me in my gender discovery, so meeting and working with them was going to be out of this world but also terrifying. Not because they were scary, but because I had so many feelings and thanks for them. It was what I could only imagine meeting Matt Baker would feel like. That, coupled with the fact that I'd never organized a whole shoot on my own before, meant that I was at death's door. Three coffees in, and an unexpected arrival from someone whom I'd once told I fancied and then proceeded to be ghosted by arriving to help out, we were ready to go. Travis was walking towards me, and I was in awe. I'd been following and digesting their work for years when I was not in London and still stuck in Dorchester, so this was a moment that I felt was full circle. Travis Alabanza was one of the first people to publicly show me that being non-binary wasn't full of constant hardship, but was actually something that was full of beauty. Something that was an addition, but not something that should detract from craft, or expertise, or skill. We were having a cigarette and waiting for Alok Vaid-Menon, the other cover star who was popping in during their European speaking tour, and they asked me how I was getting on. We knew each other from social media but had never really had an opportunity to actually speak.

I will never forget what they told me. They told me to remember what it is that I love doing, and never forget why I love doing it, but to make sure that as a gender non-conform-ing person, I don't become pigeon-holed by that narrative for the rest of my working life. That gender non-conforming people are more than that. That we are actually able to have a skilled craft that doesn't have to explicitly be about being non-binary. We should be able to choose when we include that in our words, and not be expected to or ushered to do so at all times.

Truthfully, at that time, it did go in one ear and out the other because I was in the infancy of navigating the media world. I hadn't experienced long-term exposure to this type of conversation and dialogue and was happy to talk about it. I actually wanted to talk about allyship because foolishly I believed that this was my prerogative and what I was 'meant to be doing' in this space. But now, Travis's words ring true to me through all that I do, and I'm eternally grateful to have heard them at that time in my life, because now I realize that it is never our duty to educate and tell people how to treat us, especially through our work. It's up to us as non-binary people to decide when we want to educate and if we want to. We should never be forced to do so, because not only does this have the ability to impact our work life and careers, but it is also a true tax on our mental health. The emotional labour to not only have to live a life as a marginalized person but then through your work discuss and bear the brunt of educating the people around you with 43,092 questions, often as an expectation rather than a choice, is too much for anyone.

Sometimes it bewilders me that people don't understand the concept of allyship, and I remember feeling very fancy and philosophical over the summer of 2019 while sitting down and thinking, is this because of one of the greatest, most evolutionary tools of our time? Instagram.

Bear with me.

Allyship has become a conversation topic that is happening daily, if not hourly, dependent on who you follow and what your social feeds look like. It's a conversation that is so intrinsically linked to performance that I fear that often the motivation for allyship has shifted. We are now in a time of performative wokeness, in which the people around us are in constant fear, ensuring that they are saying and sharing and preaching the right things. Part of me wonders if these people are even doing the work themselves. We see people sharing and discussing such monumental social topics online so often that it often becomes a discussion around whether people are just discussing these topics for clout. Or worse, for followers. This is only a part of what I see online. Social media and the ways in which we can influence and discuss lived experience and the nuance of a marginalized existence to tens of thousands of people is something I am eternally grateful for. It's one of the best ways for me to not only share tips on allyship when I feel fit to, but to also be an ally to the people around me. Sharing their work, uplifting their messages, ensuring people go to their shows, buying their work as independent queer businesses, and generally signposting people to other grassroots groups, or charities, that help us continue our education and growth. It's also a great opportunity for me to un-learn socialized behaviour. But that shouldn't be where it stops. That should be, if anything, a catalyst to do more, all the time. We all have lives to listen to, people to care for and groups that need us to be there for them. Just because we are marginalized does not mean that there are not other people suffering from the same dull weight above us all. Our identities aren't just tribes; they're interconnected. Weaving in and out of each other, rather beautifully, across communities and across continents.

Sharing pictures and words of queer people or people of colour or disabled people on your social media networks but still not actively doing anything in real life to ensure the spaces that we exist within are accessible is performative wokeness at its peak. It's the equivalent of being out for a meal and topping up only your glass of water when it's empty and not the person's you're with. It's self-serving.

But then who does it come down to to get people to be allies? Is it *our* job? Do we just wait for people to become allies? Is it a hybrid of the two?

Unfortunately we are in a time now in the UK especially where transphobic rhetoric and discussions targeting gender non-conforming and non-binary people are at an all-time high. TERF (trans exclusionary radical feminism) activity is a pandemic within our own community, and it's only getting stronger and more organized. The formation of the LGB Alliance in 2019 saw genuine terror and realization set into so many trans siblings of mine, as well as in me, at how vociferous these people are and are going to continue to be. The endorsement of their views and bile coming from national media means that their poisonous words are being validated, offering the trans people that these words affect nowhere to hide. Many of the UK's biggest and most prominent journalists and broadcasters, all the way down to our magical authors and shit comedians, are aligning themselves with this toxic group, all in the name of protecting the definition and rights of 'biology'.

The very notion of this 'debate', but also so often, our own literal existence, is not only transphobic but also another example of how binary the world we live in is. Aside from gender, we exist in a time where we are either right or wrong. It's yes or no. We are continually made to have to go back and forth, debating whether or not trans people are allowed to have access to basic necessities. To respect, and to kindness. This potent debate that exists around transness is a movement that has blood on its hands. To deny existence is to act as if we never existed. To continually remove our rich history, and instead in its place, leave emptiness, and in that emptiness, lies and mistruths fill the gap, creating an image that was never true. Expungement from society. No records of our existence, because when it comes down to it, the people who are in charge don't want us to be here.

So who should be doing the work to allow us to be seen? Is it us, the experts on our existence? Or is it our allies, being able to help elevate our voices into spaces and environments that aren't always accessible to us? It's a conversation that seems to be going around in concentric circles, and truthfully, I still am unsure as to where I stand on the subject, specifically the movement towards the oppressed educating the oppressor. The conversation is moving in a way that is both allowing non-binary people to not have to constantly do the leg work, but is also meaning that cis people are failing to educate themselves because there's a lack of empathy or care behind their motivations to learn. It's a space for non-binary people to regain the power of telling and speaking their truth, but often at the expense of their mental health and for 'trauma porn' rather than real care. Social media is an outlet to get 'likes', rather than to actually encourage people to stop and think and re-access their relationship with allyship. Again, it's performative wokeness. The motivation to educate and become an ally often doesn't come from witnessing and hearing the hardships of non-binary people but from wanting to ensure that you're 'ahead of the curve' and publicly and socially seen to be advocating for our rights to exist and, more than that, thrive. Hence why it then often falls back down to us. Or, it comes with trans people having to literally stand on stage, cry a bit, trawl through some of their most traumatic experiences on this planet, for a white middle-aged mum to maybe well up a little, and then decide that she should care a bit because her friend Susan's brother's stepson's child is trans.

★

My TEDxLondonWomen's talk was one of the most terrifying experiences of my life. I was asked in September 2019 to speak at their annual event, in its second year, in December, in front of just under a thousand people. One thousand eyes, ears and brains, all listening to what I would have to say, and then further thousands when it was shared online. A career highlight, but also an experience that, at the beginning, presented me with two options. I could either speak about the truth of my experiences, the harshness of trans existence, the pain, the trauma. Or I could talk about the joy. The frivolity. The self-nourishment that being trans has the capacity to drown us in. The complete joy of just being able to be ourselves. I started with the latter but realized that what I was writing wasn't true. I couldn't just 'be myself'. I wasn't able to just 'be', and writing that on paper and subsequently speaking it aloud didn't sit right with me. This was a moment when I had the autonomy to decide what I would speak about. There is a power that comes with choice. A power that allows your words to be ignited by passion, and truth, and confidence. I wasn't being funnelled into a little box by being asked to speak about the oppression I and my community face. I very carefully chose to speak about my journey and my experiences in a way that highlighted that terror but that also painted a picture of a joy that I once had. A joy that had been lost, through no fault of my own. To create a scene that showed the potential that trans people all around us have but aren't always allowed to tap into because of continual societal pressure.

After my talk, what surprised me was the questions I received. I was trotted out into the lobby of Queen Elizabeth Hall in London to meet the audience, speak with them and hear feedback on my talk. I was allocated two minders who were on hand to deal with any awkward or uncomfortable questions. We had devised a plan that if I were to be with someone who was asking me an intense question that I didn't particularly want to answer, I would rub my ear. Ten minutes later and my ear was practically bleeding. My hand never left it. Person after person would come over, congratulate me on my talk, fawn over the stars on my face, only to then ask, *'When you say be active allies and stand up and speak up for the trans community, what do you actually mean? What does that actually look like?'*

Don't get me wrong, it's a partly valid question. Allyship can often feel like something that we understand figuratively, but in action we don't know how to visualize it. Most people realize that allyship takes many forms. Financial, emotional, mental, physical, and their humanity and general normality kicks in and they understand how to be decent human beings. But what I hear and feel when person after person asks me that question is, *'How do you be a good person?'* If, after hearing a trans person speak about the reasons behind allyship being so necessary and their own experiences with a lack of care from other people, you still feel the need to come up to us and ask us how or why it's important, then that's when I clock out. My shift is well and truly over.

One cis straight white man came over and congratulated me on the talk. He wasn't making any eye contact and I couldn't tell if he was shy or embarrassed or wanted to fuck me. Probably all three. About ten seconds into the conversation, he very casually explained to me that he didn't understand my identity and continued to go on the defensive about how his upbringing and his own cis, heteronormative, 'classic' lifestyle meant that he just didn't understand. As if I were to then have to console him for his privilege. As if it was actually my fault that I was so bizarre, that my identity was in fact alienating the 'normal' people, and I should have a bit more leeway with cis straight men. My hand immediately went to my ear. If I could have, I would've pulled my ear lobe off and given it to one of my minders and popped outside to chain smoke, looking through the window to see this man get even more blush in the face than me. I felt deflated. In my eighteen-month work life, this had been one of the highlights of my career. The thought of the hard work, tears and emotional turmoil, truth be told, that went into that talk, only for me to then be greeted by ignorance immediately after, made my piss boil. I listened to him and told him that this wasn't the time. I explained that I wasn't going to sit there and explain my identity and that's not what the talk was about. It wasn't a justification of my existence; it was a call to action. For our community's plight not to be lost, and ignored, and turned into numbers on a memorial list. For black trans women to not have to spend their year grieving or worrying that their name will be next. For trans people to be able to remember the joy that they once had and for other people to support and celebrate that joy. I sent Joe Bloggs on his merry way and went outside for a cigarette. Sometimes you can't win. Even if you feel like you've done a good job, there will always be people who put their own fragility before wanting to accept that they might need to be just that little bit better.

I find media a belligerently frustrating industry to work within as a non-binary trans person for two reasons. The first being that often you are asked to write about awful things. 'A trans person has been denied [insert basic human right here]. Do you want to tell people why this is bad?' or '[insert white comedian/journalist/man] has claimed that he identifies as a [insert inanimate object here]. Tell us why this is also bad.' I used to take all of those jobs and instantly say yes, purely because I a) didn't know better and b) needed to pay my rent. But I also took the jobs because I think sometimes we can evoke change in some of the situations we are put in, even though they can also can result in disaster. TV, radio, all of these situations where we are asked to come on and speak about a topical news piece can have both positive and negative reactions and results with the viewer. It can allow trans people to see someone speaking up for more than just a 'cause', but for something that trans people feel and face every single day. To see someone potentially telling millions of people about trans-specific lived experience can sometimes feel like a eureka moment. You want to shout 'YES, FINALLY' sometimes when seeing transness discussed in a positive, non-didactic way.

But it can also create too much of a magnifying glass on the trans community. If trans people simply said no to doing such media ventures, then often the segment would be cut or spoken about so poorly that even Joe Bloggs would be able to realize that they're just talking codswallop. It's often not a clear-cut scenario, and the question I am always pondering in my head when asked to do these types of things is, *'Yeah but what if I say no, and they then just have transphobes discussing trans people with no one to even offer a credible alternative?'* But that's not our life purpose; it's a decision, like so many we make in the world, as to whether or not we want to engage. What we should be doing is supporting and looking after the people who do decide to do these types of jobs, whilst directing them to really think about whether or not the opportunity is to discuss existence or actual change. Even if the end result is not what we hoped for, our priority should be to look after our own first, at all times.

★

Just before I moved to university, I had to do a research project over the summer that was literally one of the most iconic research tasks of all time. It essentially asked me to go to London, take photos and review all of the huge department stores, and then form this into a presentation, discussing my favourite parts of Liberty or Harrods. What an absolute treat. I remember it was the first time that I'd come to London on my own, and I was staying with my sister Beth who was living in South London, so met her in the centre of the city and we made our way to her flat where she was living with her boyfriend. We got on the Tube, and she'd just been to a hilariously fancy dinner and was in all of her finery, which included a little '60s dress, filling out at the waist and falling down into a little flowery skirt. Sensational. Sadly she was wearing a kitten heel, but I guess not everyone in my bloodline has the sensibility to understand that heels below four inches are just flats, and we will forgive her for that.

We got onto the underground, and I remember it was quiet, but there were two or three young men sat in the carriage we were getting onto. We strolled on and walked past them to find seats at the next set of uncomfortable stones of concrete that Transport for London decides to call 'seats'. As we walked by, one of them wolf whistled my sister, and they all started jeering and laughing. As their wolf whistle remained in orbit around the carriage, I stopped. Disgusted by what I'd just heard, and potentially because of the adrenaline from my maiden solo voyage to London, I was full of some form of gusto and called them out. What I actually did was tell them to shut the fuck up and that they were disgusting. But with that, they did actually shut the fuck up. I don't know if it was because I was so firm, and no one normally calls out that behaviour, as I've come to realize since living in London for four years. Someone could literally be doing a shit in front of you on the Tube and no one would even glance over their copies of this book they've astily bought upon release to see what's happening. Me and my sister continued down the carriage and sat down, and nothing was said. She half giggled, but that's Beth. She's not really one to draw attention to herself or make a scene. A woman who is very careful with her words, and doesn't use more than necessary. Clearly the juxtaposition of that gene went into my body. I was an ally to my sister, but at this point I didn't really realize it. I was just sticking up for her, in a time when if she was alone she would've been vulnerable and needed it. It just felt right. An act that didn't really need thought. Fight or flight.

Often in public, people are terrified of confrontation. They'd rather die than actively get involved in someone else's drama, despite the fact that when someone is having a juicy conversation in a coffee shop, we are *all* the first to take out one earphone and pause our music and nosey in on Tracey's Avon dramas. We love being nosey without ever fully launching ourselves in. That would be too much. That would be prying. But that's exactly what happens, especially when it's society's most vulnerable who bear the brunt of this kind of reaction. We are left to fight on our own, especially in public spaces, and this is an incredibly dangerous position to be in. We don't have anywhere to go. The people around us aren't helping, and our services and police forces are institutionally set up to not care or to vilify us because of the colour of our skin, or to say that because our identities aren't 'widely recognized', that they don't have enough 'stats' or 'information' to be able to fully be there for us as a resource. We make up the numerous people who are silenced by inactivity.

After university, a few friends and I moved just six miles away to Wimbledon, which felt adult enough for us because it was closer to London and because we were able to graduate and move out without having to take that terrifying step of moving back in with our parents. We did it. We were doing life...kind of. One Sunday, I made the twenty-minute trip into town and began my Sunday ritual of having coffee and rapidly realizing nobody answers emails at the weekend (quite rightly), and sitting there for far too long debating whether or not this should be a job I aspired to or if I should just get a 'normal' job and conform to the 9–5. It was all getting a bit much, so I popped outside for a cigarette to clear my head. Everyone always tells me to not leave my possessions, including my laptop and bag and more importantly my makeup bag in public places, but I'd decided that it was fine. Once I actually managed to leave all of my belongings in the same place for nearly an hour because I nipped out for a cigarette and decided it would be a good time to get some bits and bobs for my bedroom, and ended up returning to the coffee shop with two reed diffusers, a new laundry basket and some fake succulent plants to find my things right where I left them.

It was August so it was still pretty warm, and I was wearing a maxi dress, which caught the breeze expertly at times that the music I was listening to warranted a dramatic peak in skirt choreography. I perched myself outside, just by the main doors, resting on the glass exterior, and began killing myself by carefully lighting one of my many sticks of death. As I was stood there, I realized a group of three men were approaching from the left. It was a busy day. There's a bus stop right opposite where I was stood, and the main Wimbledon train station was just over the road, as was the middle of the high street, so it was a populated area full of people being healthy on a Sunday as well as people getting absolutely drunk for no other reason than it's Sunday. Fine. I think if you're in any way someone who presents femme to the world, you are always hyperaware of every man that ever walks past you. We just have that hypervigilance of 'Oh, okay, there's a man'. Even if it's for no reason, we're just aware that they're there and are walking past. Or are stood in front of us.

The three men came closer into view, and I realized that they were drunk. One of them was carrying a blue plastic bag that now appeared vacuum-packed into a cylinder due to the weight of the bottle inside. Much like the femme person's hypervigilance of men, you are also hyperaware of when something could go awry. That feeling of holding your breath and just letting people walk past. Or when you're walking home and you see a group of men that you know you have to walk past, so you hold your breath and shrink your shoulders into yourself. Catapult your head down, as if these actions are suddenly going to turn you invisible and you're going to be able to seamlessly stroll past, with no attention drawn. No words said. No actions taken. As they approached, I did just that. Looked the other way, smoking in that direction, as if to purposefully ensure that I didn't show any signs of engagement with them. But looking away was to my detriment. When they approached from my left side, with my head right, smoke in my eyes and music blaring, I was unaware that they were now stood next to me, talking to me. I took one headphone out, turned the volume down and listened to what they had to say. It wasn't really all that clear what they were actually saying, due to the slurring and potential hint of an accent, but I didn't say anything. I remained nonchalant. In these situations when people engage with me, I still actively try my hardest to remain in my prior position. Ignoring them. Putting my head down, not making any eye contact, just showing them hard and clear signs that I don't want to be spoken to. However, here that didn't quite go to plan. Although my headphones were back in my ears the music was paused and I was listening into their conversation.

'What the fuck is it?' one of the men slurred to the other, as my head was still facing the other direction. Giving them eye contact felt too much of an engagement for conversation, or worse, action, so I remained head to the side. People streamed off the bus opposite me, but I didn't ask for help. Maybe I should have? Maybe if I'd shot them a glance it would've stopped?

'I don't fucking know, what's under there?'

Out of the corner of my eye I realized that one of them was gesturing to my skirt. I froze. I knew where this was going. I knew exactly what was about to happen. But I was frozen still. Why the fuck was I still? Why didn't I just put my cigarette out and go inside? Leave. Escape.

The man with the bag bent down and put his hands up my skirt. The skirt fell to my shins, so he was crouched low and flipped the end of my skirt over his head and proceeded to put his hands on my thighs. I was still frozen. Another bus arrived. Another mass of busy people getting from A to B. Rapidly walking home to the warmth of an open front door.

I finally moved. Raising my right leg, I kneed the man off of me. As he recoiled, I threw another kick into his stomach and he fell backwards, not fully, but enough to wobble off kilter into the middle of the street. I knew this was it. This was the moment it was either over and they were going to leave, or this was just the beginning. Fortunately I was no longer frozen, and I walked in the opposite direction once I'd decided to kick him in the stomach with a four-inch boot. Shaking, I walked away, stopping just a few metres away to see if they were following or if they had decided to skulk away. They were all now walking in the opposite direction, probably too drunk to even realize what had happened, clutching each other in tandem as they crossed the road towards the station.

I looked around me. There were tens, if not hundreds of people congregating after sitting on stuffy buses in this bizarre August heat. I returned to my spot, unsure what to do. I think when things like this happen you just kind of presume that people will come over and ask if you're okay. Or you presume that someone must have seen what had happened. This all occurred not only with a busy outside presence of people bustling around, but against the glass wall of an equally busy coffee shop. But no one came over. Does that mean people hadn't seen? No. But did anyone who did see care enough to come over? No. People continued on their missions to get home, heads down, music on. I stood there and began shouting. Expletives mostly, but the one thing I remember shouting, apart from, 'What the fuck just happened?' was actually a sarcastic cry of, 'OH YES, I'M FINE, THANK YOU VERY MUCH', to which still no one bothered to enquire.

I realized that I was just stood there shouting, so I decided to go inside. I still was in shock, not just at what had happened but at the fact that I'd actively just kicked a stranger in the chest. Thinking about whether or not I was going to get in trouble, doubting whether or not I was a good person. Turning it on myself instantly, seeing myself as the problem. Surely they would've seen what had happened. I'd developed a rapport with the staff now, so I returned to my seat expecting at least some questioning as to what had just happened outside. I sat down and nothing was said. The coffee machine in front of me continued to whirl and splutter, and people continued to read their books, chat with their boring boyfriends and spend all of their money on overpriced juice. That was it. This reaction in part made me think, had I just made the whole thing up? Did that actually happen, or was this a figment of my imagination? Because surely if this *had* happened, someone would've a) seen and b) then at least asked if I was okay. But apparently not.

On the walk home, I reluctantly rang the police. I have

never really trusted the police, especially when it comes to queer issues, and since learning about the intrinsic bias and failures of the police force in the UK and the US, they were actually the last people I wanted to speak to. But after thinking about it, I realized that this seemed like the logical thing to do. A formality. A thing people do. I'm people, I should do that. I rang them and they asked repeatedly what happened. 'What type of dress were you wearing, sir? How long was the skirt, sir?' he probed, almost sounding like the very men whom I had encountered a few hours prior. 'Thank you, sir, make a note of your case number and someone will ring you shortly about attending your house for a visit within the next two to three days. Thank you, sir, goodbye.' A tepid response when what I needed was warmth. Apologies for what had happened, yet a clear lack of understanding about who this had happened to and what the ramifications of such an incident would be for a person like myself.

They came two days later. I let the policeman into my house, again wary of all men, just as I was on that Sunday. He sat down in the living room in front of a picture of a woman rubbing oil and thyme leaves into her boobs. He just seemed to nod at the picture, as if it could respond. Again I recalled the event. When it happened. Where it happened. Who it was. What they looked like. Ignoring his leading questions regarding the race of the attackers and whether or not they 'looked homeless'. Then he asked if there were any witnesses. Truthfully, I didn't really know how to answer this one. Because yes there were, but no there weren't. There were passive witnesses. Bystanders, watching this unfold, and although the incident was a maximum of five seconds long, someone definitely saw. I explained this to him, and he came back with some flabby answer about how 'that's just Londoners for you', as if living in a city like London means that you're apparently unable to form any measure of empathy or care for another human being's life and you instead just shrug off sexual assault as something commonplace. As something normal. That's not the London I knew, but swiftly became the city I now breathe within.

He left. I hadn't told anyone what happened personally. I shared what had happened on social media, leaving out the details, and focusing primarily on where to go when things like this happen, because when these things do happen it's often so disorientating that the logical part of your brain doesn't work. It goes into overdrive, and the things that you think you would do in that instance don't seem like logical things to do. It's very easy to sit outside of a situation, as we all do, and say what you would do in that instance. But being there is a whole different kettle of fish. Three days later the policeman rang me back, and told me that he'd been to the coffee shop and asked to see their CCTV. He had also acquired the CCTV footage of the high street that it happened on, even asking to see CCTV from the buses that had been parked there whilst the attack happened. He found nothing. The only flicker of evidence was a view of the three men walking down the road ten minutes before, when they were making their way down to the centre of Wimbledon.

'I'm sorry, but we've now closed the case. Thanks for your time, and you know where we are if you need to speak to us again. Goodbye, sir.'

★

Allyship starts with empathy and compassion. Empathy that takes you out of yourself and just for a second puts you into the shoes of someone else. It's something we are currently so lacking as a human race. Being in their shoes. It's the feeling and notion of taking our neo-liberalist hats off and stepping into the world as someone else with the aim and motivation to make their life easier. To make their experiences easier and more accessible. If someone had had more empathy in those instances when we were attacked, our lives would've potentially taken a different path. If someone had come over and asked if I was okay, we wouldn't have to learn how to deal with trauma in ways that lead to more. Just a hug, that can be all it takes sometimes to show that you're there and you're present. Who knows, maybe then we won't have to take such drastic action when it comes to the harmful and omnipresent methods of distraction and avoidance that often come with being victims of abuse, especially sexual abuse. This happens all over the world, to non-binary and gender non-conforming people on a day-to-day basis, and for some reason it goes unchallenged. Countless times we are mocked, laughed at, trolled and vilified both in our physical life as well as within our online communities, yet we are passed the baton to stand up for ourselves and fight against groups of people who have only the intention of bringing us down.

5 THINGS I'D SAY TO PEOPLE WANTING TO BE AN ALLY

1. Check your privilege. Just because you're part of a marginalized community doesn't mean that you can't be an ally. Being queer doesn't mean that you're not complicit within other institutional power structures, such as racism, Islamophobia, ableism, anti-Semitism, etc.

2. Don't rely on the marginalized person to constantly be your educator. Unless you're paying that person, or that person or group has allowed themselves to dedicate time to the subject, don't just ask marginalized people how to treat them with kindness, empathy and compassion.

3. Educate yourself. Many non-binary people had to educate themselves through social media and online resources on the very notion and history of what being non-binary is, so the least that you can do is actively do the same as an ally. Read the books, find the online spaces and remember to not take up too much space as an ally in these communities.

4. De-centre yourself from the conversation. For example, as white people often our white fragility and lack of awareness when it comes to race can feel to some like an attack on you as a person. But knowing that this isn't about your feelings as a white person and is more about knowing how we are complicit within institutional racism, and more so how we can start the continual journey to ensuring that we stamp out and erase these practices in our day-to-day, is the most important thing we need to be doing.

5. Despite what a lot of people will tell you, it's okay to get things wrong. But it's not okay to continually be wrong. Being called out or told that what you've done is wrong, again, similarly to point four, isn't about you. It's not a time for you to whine about your feelings being hurt; it's a time when you need to accept you were wrong and continue about your life ensuring you don't make the same mistakes. Once is fine, twice is not.

There's a common misconception that queerness and transness means that we are unable to be complicit in other oppressive situations. Being queer or trans or non-binary does not mean that we do not also need to do the work. As a white queer non-binary person who works within the media, it is clear to me that a lot of the opportunities and work that I do acquire is a) because I have interesting makeup that people want to stare at but also b) because I'm white and thin. That's deemed by them as a more 'palatable' way to digest queerness, implying that queer black and brown people are just 'too complicated' or 'too rare' to care about. That their stories and lives aren't worthy of care or celebration. Our queer and trans siblings of colour need our allyship now more than ever, and it's our job to ensure that we are looking out for our own community's most marginalized, especially if we are in a position of privilege within our community.

I have been to countless events and talks that are focused around trans/non-binary people yet there have not been provisions made for people with physical access requirements, therefore they can't attend. For example, London Pride and many other organizations that hold events have had issues with ensuring that everybody is able to attend and enjoy the celebrations, and that they aren't excluded just because they're in a wheelchair or have mental health issues that mean they don't enjoy crowds or busy spaces. These issues are often disregarded or not seen as primary issues, so these people within our own community are unable to access the exact same events that their able-bodied counterparts can. How are we supposed to stand as a united front to cis people when often our own queer spaces can't even be accessible and show allyship to members of their own rainbow-clad group?

After the attack, I vowed never to talk about allyship again. When I shared the situation on social media, click-bait queer news sites took the story and ran it without my consent, meaning that a situation that had just happened twenty-four hours earlier was now being shared with millions of people without my consent. I then wrote about this experience, but also about the attack itself, for *Gay Times*, and declared mentally to myself that this was the last time that I was going to publicly talk about allyship and centre it in my conversations. Truly, because I was tired of it. I was tired of having to basically beg people to treat our community with respect, specifically after having been attacked. Having the catalyst for this discussion be an attack on my body, and on my being, really showed me that people only care after something has happened. When the Pulse Orlando shooting happened, suddenly there was an outpouring of support and care for our community; quite rightly so. But why wasn't it there before? Why didn't we have the radical support of our cis-het community prior to a deadly tragedy? I do speak about allyship now, but in a more direct and actively angry way. Anger is such a strong emotion that non-binary people often feel, and sometimes it's useful. Sometimes it's important to have anger, because that's often when we really shift our discussions up a gear, and away from a lucid panel discussion, into real action.

For the past three years, I've been sitting on panels, going to shoots and speaking to people about allyship, and it's time for us to stop pushing that as our constant message. As non-binary people, there's only so much that we can say about how we need you to help us. It's not our job to tell cis people how to treat non-binary people with respect. Take our words as a marker of time, and a marker of history, and realize that what we have said before still stands today. Speaking about allyship often feels like screaming but nothing is coming out. Like those weird, fanatical dreams that we often have where we are in turmoil and we are screaming, running around asking for help, but for some reason no one can hear us. But this time it's real. It's a feeling and a state of being that should be linked through all of the conversations and interactions that we have, every single day. It's an adaptation of our day-to-day, to ensure that we are making the lives of those around us easier. Allyship isn't just something that's going to stop me from getting misgendered, it's a tool that shows the communities that you apply it to that you're there for us. You're there, on this journey. That you know that allyship and unlearning societal behaviours isn't a tick box but a process that you will carry out for the rest of your life. A constant process of evaluation and then action. It's adaptable to the climates that those people are in, and especially now, trans and non-binary people need your allyship. Urgency doesn't even cover the magnitude of what we are facing across the world, and soon we won't be able to stand up and fight for ourselves and our communities anymore because we will be gone and it will be too late.

As a human race, we are all in this together, and picking people up when they are down and being by their side when they need that extra bit of support should be instinctive. The next time you see something that makes you uncomfortable in public or online, remember the silence that the victim can hear when no one comes to their side. Remember the vulnerability and loneliness that encompasses all of the violence that non-binary people face, day in, day out. The next time you see it, stand up, step in and be by our side. Provide humanity, not because you're a hero, but because you're human.

Take the Weight off Your Feet

I've always found time weird. People always ask me what I'm going to look like when I'm sixty, and truthfully there will be no amount of ageing or wrinkling that would stop me from wearing copious amounts of blush alongside my neat set of stars. But as I grow older and time lurks around me, I hope that when I'm sixty we are in a time when we are able to breathe. Able to relax a bit more. That when I am old and grey, and bald still, that we are able to look at this time that we are in and crack out a slight smile. A smirk that says, '*Well fucking done.*' To be able to look back at the hardships we are in now, the fights, the pain, tenderness and say, '*We got there.*'

I have so much hope for the generation coming behind me. It feels weird to say that because I still feel like a toddler, but over the past three years we have seen some of the most impassioned and fiery action from our youngest members of society. From climate change to Brexit, our young people are some of the most engaged members of society, and that is something that fills me with the most hope. A hope that we can continue what we are all fighting for now. No matter how small, our voices are being carried by a generation of people who aren't willing to allow the status quo to continue, and I am so proud of that. So proud of the young trans people who exist in the world, not allowing their futures to become filled with mottled memories that will stay with them forever, but knowing that they are fully invested in preserving and highlighting their truest sense of self for the rest of their lives.

For me, self-appreciation and self-celebration is something I am fervently going to work towards. I have just started therapy, and it's been like someone tapping me on my glasses and saying, '*Excuse me, take care of yourself, you're precious. Allow yourself to care for yourself sometimes.*' My first therapy session was absolutely terrifying and consisted of me sitting opposite a man that I definitely decided that I fancied and having to just start talking about my life, rather than being quizzed on it, as therapy is depicted in the films. I also felt so bad for speaking about myself for an hour that at the end I apologized for not saying '*and you?*' Speaking about your life, your hardships, your brilliance, your joy aloud puts it into perspective. Hearing your words and your life played back to you by a somewhat sexy therapist is often a way to hear what you've not wanted to hear for so long. Whether it be good or bad, hearing what you're essentially living is like being shown the sitcom of your life. You can't look away. You can't stop listening to what's being said, questioning whether or not this sexy stranger opposite you is actually talking about you. But they are. You are both there to make yourself better, and caring for yourself in whatever way possible is something we all need to put at the top of our lists going forward. We can only try and better ourselves in this life, and taking the step to do that is so crucial.

Non-binary people reading this, I want you to know that I love you. Our journeys, our lives, our loves are so instilled in all of us that hearing each other's stories can feel like putting on your favourite pair of slippers. A comfortable feeling, grounding you to the earth that we are walking upon. A feeling that allows you to stop holding your breath, fully exhaling.

We are in a time now when the fight against us is so

strategic and planned that we need to come together first, as a community, to ensure that we are so tightly knit and impenetrable that anything that is thrown at us just ricochets off instantly. Be there for our non-binary siblings of colour, our non-binary homeless people, our trans disabled people. Our fight is their fight. We are an amalgamation of the intricacies of our own community, and our power and our fight comes from those nuances. We are the sum of our own parts.

I have cried so many times writing this, sat with a banoffee-flavoured cocktail, just writing, and crying, and deleting, and writing, trying to make sure I am making an ounce of sense. But I realized swiftly that it's okay to just say what needs to be said. It's okay to be raw. It's okay to let go. So often we feel like we have to live up to a standard that isn't realistic, and we owe it to ourselves to say 'FUCK THAT' and exist to our own standards. Set your own barometers of success, of gender euphoria, of frivolity, of freedom. Our lives can feel so precarious and often floating out of reality that we truly owe it to ourselves to be our own arbitrators of what we need and what we don't. Allow yourself, unapologetically, to desire and need things that will help you grow. People will tell you you're selfish, or stupid, or wrong, or dramatic. But know that you're not. Asking for things that will help you be your best self is never something that is wrong or foolish.

As I sit here, tears running down my face, waitresses looking at me thinking that I've lost the absolute plot, I thank you from the bottom of my heart. I love you. I believe in you, because we have to. Hold each other's hands tight and know that you're going to be okay. Know that everything is yours for the taking. Our identities, our beauty in our bespokeness, is never, ever, something to apologize for.

Ask for help when you need it, and know that there is always, *always*, a community here for you. No matter how small it may feel at times, it's always here for you, arms outstretched, ready to bring you in and embrace you. Remember to breathe. In and out, each day at a time, one step at a time, with your best foot forward. No one can replace you in this life, and being non-binary is never something that you have to change about yourself, ever. It's something that will feel like a weight on your chest as well as a crown on your head. Wear it with pride. Let it shine and allow it to glisten atop you. I am so proud of you. We are so proud of you, forever. Forever we will continue to rise, like we have been doing since the dawn of time, as a force that is never-ending. Never forget that power that you have, for it's yours. Cherish it, and hold on to it, and remember to breathe.